CHALLENGE

ATTITUDE ADJUSTMENT

AT A GLANCE

D1227063

Serendipity House / P.O. Box 1012 / Littleton, CO 80160

TOLL FREE 1-800-525-9563 / www.serendipityhouse.com

© 1989, 1998 Serendipity House. All rights reserved.

SECOND EDITION

98 99 00 01 / **201 series • CHG** / 4 3

PROJECT ENGINEER:
Lyman Coleman

WRITING TEAM:
Richard Peace, Lyman Coleman, Matthew Lockhart, Andrew Sloan, Cathy Tardif

PRODUCTION TEAM:
Christopher Werner, Sharon Penington, Erika Tiepel

COVER PHOTO:
© 1998 Michael Powers / Adventure Photo and Film

CORE VALUES

Community: The purpose of this curriculum is to build community within the body of believers around Jesus Christ.

Group Process: To build community, the curriculum must be designed to take a group through a step-by-step process of sharing your story with one another.

Interactive Bible Study: To share your "story," the approach to Scripture in the curriculum needs to be open-ended and right brain—to "level the playing field" and encourage everyone to share.

Developmental Stages: To provide a healthy program in the life cycle of a group, the curriculum needs to offer courses on three levels of commitment: (1) Beginner Stage—low-level entry, high structure, to level the playing field; (2) Growth Stage—deeper Bible study, flexible structure, to encourage group accountability; (3) Discipleship Stage—in-depth Bible study, open structure, to move the group into high gear.

Target Audiences: To build community throughout the culture of the church, the curriculum needs to be flexible, adaptable and transferable into the structure of the average church.

ACKNOWLEDGMENTS

To Zondervan Bible Publishers
for permission to use
the NIV text,
The Holy Bible, New International Bible Society.
© 1973, 1978, 1984 by International Bible Society.
Used by permission of Zondervan Bible Publishers.

Questions & Answers

STAGE

1. What stage in the life cycle of a small group is this course designed for?

Turn to the first page of the center section of this book. There you will see that this 201 course is designed for the second stage of a small group. In the Serendipity "Game Plan" for the multiplication of small groups, your group is in the Growth Stage.

GOALS

2. What are the goals of a 201 study course?

As shown on the second page of the center section (page M2), the focus in this second stage is equally balanced between Bible Study, Group Building, and Mission / Multiplication.

BIBLE STUDY

3. What is the approach to Bible Study in this course?

Take a look at page M3 of the center section. The objective in a 201 course is to discover what a book of the Bible, or a series of related Scripture passages, has to say to our lives today. We will study each passage seriously, but with a strong emphasis on practical application to daily living.

THREE-STAGE LIFE CYCLE OF A GROUP

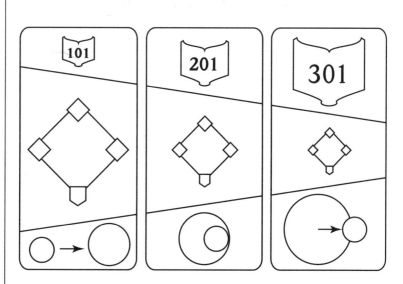

GROUP BUILDING

4. *What is the meaning of the baseball diamond on pages M2 and M3 in relation to Group Building?*

Every Serendipity course includes group building. First base is where we share our own stories; second base means affirming one another's stories; third base is sharing our personal needs; and home plate is deeply caring for each others' needs. In this 201 course we will continue "checking in" with each other and holding each other accountable to live the Christian life.

MISSION / MULTIPLICATION

5. *What is the mission of a 201 group?*

The mission of this 201 Covenant group is to discover the future leaders for starting a new group. (See graph on the previous page.) During this course, you will be challenged to identify three people and let this team use the Bible Study time to practice their skills. The center section will give you more details.

THE EMPTY CHAIR

6. *How do we fill the "empty chair"?*

First, pull up an empty chair during the group's prayer time and ask God to bring a new person to the group to fill it. Second, have everyone make a prospect list of people they could invite and keep this list on their refrigerator until they have contacted all those on their list.

AGENDA

7. *What is the agenda for our group meetings?*

A three-part agenda is found at the beginning of each session. Following the agenda and the recommended amount of time will keep your group on track and will keep the three goals of Bible Study, Group Building, and Mission / Multiplication in balance.

THE FEARLESS FOURSOME!

If you have more than seven people at a meeting, Serendipity recommends you divide into groups of 4 for the Bible Study. Count off around the group: "one, two, one, two, etc."—and have the "ones" move quickly to another room for the Bible Study. Ask one person to be the leader and follow the directions for the Bible Study time. After 30 minutes, the Group Leader will call "Time" and ask all groups to come together for the Caring Time.

ICE-BREAKERS

8. *How do we decide what ice-breakers to use to begin the meetings?*

Page M7 of the center section contains an index of ice-breakers in four categories: (1) those for getting acquainted in the first session or when a new person comes to a meeting; (2) those for the middle sessions to help you report in to your group; (3) those for the latter sessions to affirm each other and assign roles in preparation for starting a new group in the future; and (4) those for evaluating and reflecting in the final session.

GROUP COVENANT

9. *What is a group covenant?*

A group covenant is a "contract" that spells out your expectations and the ground rules for your group. It's very important that your group discuss these issues—preferably as part of the first session.

GROUND RULES

10. *What are the ground rules for the group?* (Check those you agree upon.)

❒ PRIORITY: While you are in the course, you give the group meetings priority.

❒ PARTICIPATION: Everyone participates and no one dominates.

❒ RESPECT: Everyone is given the right to their own opinion and all questions are encouraged and respected.

❒ CONFIDENTIALITY: Anything that is said in the meeting is never repeated outside the meeting.

❒ EMPTY CHAIR: The group stays open to new people at every meeting.

❒ SUPPORT: Permission is given to call upon each other in time of need—even in the middle of the night.

❒ ADVICE GIVING: Unsolicited advice is not allowed.

❒ MISSION: We agree to do everything in our power to start a new group as our mission (see center section).

Introduction to Sermon on the Mount

Well-Known … But Neglected

The Sermon on the Mount (Matt. 5:1–7:29), like the Ten Commandments, is one of the best-known passages in the Bible. Many people are at least somewhat familiar with the Beatitudes, the Lord's Prayer, the admonition to "consider the lilies of the field," and the parable about the two men who built their houses on sand and on rock.

Yet the Sermon on the Mount is undoubtedly much better known than it is understood or practiced! Often a person will casually remark, "Well, I think all we have to do is live by the teachings in the Sermon on the Mount and we'll be okay with God." Such an offhand statement that assumes the Sermon is merely a rehash of basic moral principles which "good" people follow anyway betrays a lack of understanding of the Sermon's call for a deep, inner righteousness that "surpasses that of the Pharisees and the teachers of the law" (Matt. 5:20). There is far more than common moral maxims here!

Other people assume the Sermon on the Mount has nothing to do with the way a Christian lives today. They believe the Sermon only applies to a future age, and see the Sermon's teachings (which seemingly stress human effort over God's grace) as having no relevance for the church. But much of what is found in the Sermon on the Mount is also found elsewhere in the teachings of Jesus and Paul. One would have to dismiss the relevancy of much of the New Testament to evade the force of this sermon!

A third view assumes the Sermon is meant to accomplish exactly the opposite of what the proponents of the first view assert! Rather than giving us a basic moral program to follow, this view teaches that the Sermon is meant to break us of any hope that we can live by the laws of God. It is meant to drive us to God for mercy and grace as we realize we cannot live up to God's stringent demands. Once we recognize this, the Sermon has done its job as the new law that leaves us broken before God, finally able to receive God's grace. The difficulty of this view is that it provides the Christian with no direction as to how one is supposed to live. What does God call us to be and do once we recognize our brokenness?

A fourth view takes the Sermon very seriously as the law of the kingdom of God as laid down by Jesus. Its teachings (or at least those sections that do not require self-mutilation!) are to be applied literally. Thus, oaths are forbidden. Divorce is permitted only for adultery. Remarriage is prohibited. The use of force is never an option. Pledging to church budgets is rejected. The difficulty with this view is that the "law" of Jesus can become far more harsh and impersonal than that of Moses. It can end up leading a person to take a legalistic approach to the very words of Jesus that were in large part directed at exposing the folly of the legalistic approach of the Pharisees!

The Sermon on the Mount is not a stringing together of moral precepts that provide good advice on how to live, nor is it a picture of life in some far off "kingdom age" that has no relevance for the church, nor is it meant simply to crush its readers into despair, nor is it a new legal code to be enforced by the church. *Rather, the Sermon on the Mount is a picture of what the inner character of the follower of Jesus in any age should be like.* In this Sermon, people come face-to-face with the radical demands of the kingdom of God brought near by the coming of Jesus. This is the manifesto of God's kingdom which "describes what human life and human community look like when they come under the gracious rule of God."[1] In this brief sermon, Matthew presents the reader with unforgettable pictures of what it means to be a follower of Jesus.

Background to the Sermon

It is commonly thought that the Gospels are biographies of Jesus, a record of the day-to-day activities of Jesus written down by authors who functioned like a modern reporter recording "just the facts." Such a view is inadequate. A closer examination of the Gospels reveals that the authors were more like editors than reporters. Using an analogy from television, they are the producers, not the camera crew; they are not simply aiming the camera at whatever action happens to be going on, but are cutting and splicing the film to create an effect. The authors of the Gospels took the stories and sayings of Jesus and presented them in various ways in order to accent various truths about Jesus' identity, his mission, and his call to discipleship.

It is important to note in this regard that the Sermon is given primarily to Jesus' disciples (5:1). The crowds are present (5:1; 7:28), but the immediate audience is those who professed allegiance to Jesus. *The Sermon is not the program one must follow in order to* **become** *a disciple, but is the way of life that is to be pursued by those who* **are** *disciples.* Like all the biblical writers, Matthew makes it clear that a relationship with God is a gift one receives by God's grace: Jesus is the light to all nations, calling upon people to receive the kingdom of God (4:17). He graciously invites people to become his disciples (4:18–22). He reaches out in love to all who call upon him in faith (8:2–3,5–7; 9:2,22,29). No one earns his way to God (19:16ff), and no one is so indebted to God that he or she is without hope (18:21–35). Salvation is a gift of God.

Those who receive the gift, however, are expected to reflect the presence of the kingdom in their lives. The Sermon on the Mount reveals what that should look like in terms of a person's attitudes and actions. It shows the reader the lifestyle God desires to develop in the community of people who are following Jesus. It sets the standard for which Christians are to reach in their attitudes and relationships. It is a high goal meant to reveal the mediocrity with which most of us are comfortable and to stir us to action. Here we have a picture of personal and social righteousness that refuses to be limited. The teachings in the Sermon are the practical outworking of God's call for his people to love God and neighbor. The lifestyle embraced in these teachings is the goal pursued by those who have been motivated and empowered by God's grace.

The Focus of the Sermon

A very rough outline of the Sermon on the Mount would be to divide it into three sections:

5:1–20: The Character of the Disciple
5:21–7:6: Examples of This Character
7:7–27: Admonitions to Pursue This Character

While such a division is obviously simplistic, it focuses our attention on the central issue of the Sermon, which is the character of the follower of Jesus. Matthew 5:20 underscores the point: the Sermon exposes the need for a righteousness which exceeds that of the scribes and Pharisees. This is not meant to belittle the Pharisees, as if they were hypocritically pretending to be something they knew perfectly well they weren't. The Pharisees *were* deeply concerned about being righteous, if one considers righteousness to be a matter of outwardly conforming to the regulations, laws and traditions which they valued.

For instance, one sect of Pharisees were known as the "Bruised and Bleeding Pharisees." These men were so concerned about holiness that they took extreme measures to protect themselves from sin. In order to avoid thoughts of lust, for example, they would blindfold themselves when out in public to avoid having to look at women! The resultant problem of bumping into things and falling led to their nickname! They were very much concerned with being righteous, but Jesus pointed out that their approach was inadequate. Although it seemed to be an extreme response to the problem of lust, it was not extreme enough! His call for people to gouge out an eye and throw it away if it led them to sin may be an intentional commentary on the ineffectiveness of the way the Bruised and Bleeding Pharisees dealt with the problem of lust. Simply closing one's eyes was not sufficient; a more radical approach was needed that would get to the heart-attitude involved.

The Sermon on the Mount is not meant to be a "new law" in the sense that Jesus was laying down new regulations for people to observe. People then (and now) did not need more rules to tell them how God wanted them to live. There were plenty of perfectly good rules already. The problem, as illustrated by the history of Israel, was that people consistently minimized or bent the rules in order to fit their interests. It was this approach to God's Law that allowed the Pharisees to assume, for instance, that since they had not actually murdered anyone they had therefore fully kept the sixth commandment. It was this approach that allowed them to assume that if a divorce could be legal, then it must be moral.

This literalistic, legalistic approach to the Law was what Jesus exposed, challenged and reformed. He had no new law to give, but called for a new heart. His concern was that his followers should have their character shaped and formed by the character of God.

Interpreting the Sermon

The variety of views about the Sermon, as well as its nature as a collection of sayings, makes the question of how to interpret specific passages a difficult one. In addition, there are other considerations that affect interpretation.

For example, the Sermon is full of images and customs that need to be understood in the light of Jesus' culture. Disciples are "the light of the world." They are not to "give dogs what is sacred." They are to "enter through the narrow gate," and to "turn the other cheek" when struck on one side. Proper application of these teachings requires a sense of what that image or custom meant in Jesus' day. For example, most North Americans today only use salt as a flavoring for food, but in Jesus' day it was also used as the means of preserving food from spoiling. That gives a different twist to the picture of Jesus' disciples as "the salt of the earth." Likewise, a new perspective on the command to turn the other cheek is gained when it is understood that this refers to the disciple's response to what was an insulting gesture, not a physical assault. The notes that accompany these studies attempt to provide this background.

A second consideration affecting interpretation is familiarity with the rabbinic style of teaching. Often, a rabbi would state a general principle and then provide "case studies" to illustrate his point. While the principle was meant to be understood as a universal maxim, its application to a particular situation was not a simple matter. It was up to the rabbi to make the application. Jesus himself employed this teaching style. For instance, in 5:39a, he asserts the principle of

nonretaliation and then, in verses 39b–42, gives four case studies that illustrate the principle.

A third factor that deeply affects interpretation is the issue of which teachings are meant to be understood literally and which are to be understood figuratively. Hyperbole, a common manner of speaking in Jesus' culture, uses exaggeration to grab attention and make a point. It makes an extreme, absolute statement but is never intended to be actually interpreted and applied absolutely. Rather, it is meant to demonstrate a strong contrast with prevailing opinion so that one's mind is forced to consider a new way of thinking about a matter.

Scholars agree that hyperbole is used in this sermon, but they disagree strongly about where and when it is used. Most people would agree that hyperbole is involved in the command to "not let your left hand know what your right hand is doing" (6:3) when one gives to the needy. This statement, which obviously could not be followed literally, is seen as a strong rebuke to the ostentatious display of almsgiving practiced by the Pharisees. However, Christians are deeply divided about whether the statements "anyone who marries the divorced woman commits adultery" (5:32) or "do not resist an evil person" (5:39) are to be understood hyperbolically or literally. Many churches interpret and apply the former command literally, prohibiting divorce and remarriage, but understand the latter figuratively, allowing their members to participate in wars against aggression. The reasons for how such decisions are made are not always clear.

There are four helpful guidelines to keep in mind in trying to discern whether or not a statement is hyperbolic:

1. *What is the context to which Jesus is speaking?* Much of the Sermon on the Mount is a sharp contrast to the traditions and practices of the Pharisees and scribes (5:20,21, 27,31,33,38,43; 6:2,5,16), which ended up justifying actions and attitudes that were deeply sinful. In those cases, it is helpful to know some of the background of the traditional practices regarding divorce, oath-taking, almsgiving, prayer, etc. to which Jesus is

presenting an alternative. The questions then become: "What are the specific abuses he is seeking to correct?" and "In what similar ways are those abuses present today?"

2. *If a person practiced this command literally, would that really deal with the inner issues involved?* Throughout the Sermon, Jesus is exposing the folly of considering righteousness as a matter of outwardly conforming to the Law and traditions. His focus is on the inner attitudes involved. Cutting out my eye will leave me blind, but will not touch my heart that lusts after what my eye has seen. Something far more radical is demanded if the root problem of sin is to be dealt with. While I may obey the admonition in 5:34 to "not swear at all" and thus refuse to take oaths, the real issue is whether or not I am a person whose word can be trusted. That, and not the external matter of whether or not one takes an oath in court, is Jesus' point here.

3. *Does the literal practice of this command square with other teachings of the Bible on the subject?* In the Sermon, Jesus is really reiterating the essence of the Old Testament call for God's people to be holy. The rest of the New Testament likewise reinforces this call. There is nothing essentially unique in the Sermon regarding the ethics or morals of the Christian life. Therefore, the rest of Scripture provides "checks and balances" on our interpretations. The call to pray in one's room with the door closed (6:6) needs to be interpreted in light of the gathered prayer of the church (seen in Acts 4:24 and in many other places).

4. *Does the literal application of this teaching square with the general ethical tenor of the Bible that puts a stress on human wholeness, love and justice?* In the Sermon, Jesus clearly stands against any form of righteousness that seeks to measure itself by external conformity to some law. His concern is with the attitudes of the heart that motivate our behavior. In spite of the literal command of 5:39, in some cases it might be more loving and just for people to stand against an evil person

than to allow him or her to harm many others. The admonition here is meant to challenge people to replace their inner desire for vengeance against those who oppose them with the better way of loving service. It is not a denial of the need and appropriateness for systems of social justice such as the courts.

The Challenge of the Sermon

All of these considerations indicate that a study of the Sermon on the Mount is a challenging task! It will stretch us intellectually and spiritually. We will be tempted at times to minimize some of the hard teachings. Sometimes we will think we have found an escape hatch by saying that a certain teaching is hyperbolic, only to find that the reality exposed by that hyperbole is far more challenging than simply conforming to the statement itself. John W. Miller, in his brief but profound study on this sermon, writes:

You who take up this study, having enlisted in this movement (of the kingdom of God) at this time, should pause at this point to reflect on your readiness. Perhaps in considering Christianity you had in mind simply joining a "church." You may not have thought of the church as a "movement" calling for radical changes in your life. Or you may have thought that Christianity was primarily a matter of believing certain dogmas. You did not realize that it is far more a call to action, a call to discipleship and sometimes hard obedience. Perhaps you thought that your main responsibility as a Christian would be to go to worship services on Sunday and live a respectable life. You did not realize that joining up would involve you in a whole new lifestyle, one that might well bring you into opposition to the "kingdoms of this world." Consider: Do you want to leave the crowd and join the disciples who follow Jesus in this radical way?[2]

[1] John Stott, *The Message of the Sermon on the Mount* (InterVarsity Press, 1978), p. 18.
[2] John W. Miller, *The Christian Way* (Herald Press, 1969), p. 21.

1 Introduction—Matthew 5:1–5

THREE-PART AGENDA

ICE-BREAKER	BIBLE STUDY	CARING TIME
15 Minutes	30 Minutes	15–45 Minutes

> **LEADER:** Be sure to read pages 3–5 in the front of this book, and go over the ground rules on page 5 with the group in this first session. See page M7 in the center section for a good ice-breaker. Have your group look at pages M1–M5 in the center section and fill out the team roster on page M5.

TO BEGIN THE BIBLE STUDY TIME
(Choose 1 or 2)

1. When a movie gets real sad, are you more likely to let the tears flow, or "keep a stiff upper lip"?

2. When was the last time you were part of a large crowd of people?

3. What is something you have "inherited" from your parents or grandparents? What is something you would like to pass along to your kids?

READ SCRIPTURE & DISCUSS
(If you don't have time for all the questions in this section, conclude the Bible Study [30 min.] by answering question #8.)

1. Who is the best teacher you had in high school? What lesson did you learn from them?

2. The Sermon on the Mount is known for its "hard sayings"— where Jesus really challenges people. How do you feel about beginning such a study?

The Beatitudes

5 *Now when he saw the crowds, he went up on a mountainside and sat down. His disciples came to him, ²and he began to teach them, saying:*

³*"Blessed are the poor in spirit,*
for theirs is the kingdom of heaven.
⁴*Blessed are those who mourn,*
for they will be comforted.
⁵*Blessed are the meek,*
for they will inherit the earth."

3. Define in your own words what it means to be "poor in spirit"?

4. What kind of mourning do you feel Jesus is talking about in verse 4 (see note on v. 4)? What causes you to mourn?

5. Who do you admire as a good example of meekness? How do they model humility?

6. Which of these first three Beatitudes do you feel most challenged by?

7. This past week, have you felt more blessed or stressed? What can you do to be more focused on God's blessings in your life?

8. In what area of your life are you feeling really "blessed"? In what area could you use some "comfort"?

P.S. At the close, pass around your books and have everyone sign the Group Directory inside the front cover.

CARING TIME

1. Has your group agreed on its group goals and covenant (see page 5 in the front of this book)?

2. Have you filled out your team roster (see page M5 in the center section)? Like any winning team, every position needs to be covered.

3. What brought you to this Bible Study and what are you hoping to get out of it?

Share prayer requests and close in prayer. Be sure to pray for "the empty chair" (p. 4).

Summary. The so-called Sermon on the Mount is the first (and longest) of five major teaching sections in Matthew. Here, Jesus focuses on the subject of the kingdom of heaven and what is involved in living as a part of it. The Sermon on the Mount is not merely a collection of general ethical principles (though it does present a profound ethic); it is a focused reflection on what is involved in living in obedience to God. This is not the only place where Jesus raises these matters. Portions of his teachings can be found elsewhere in the Gospels.

5:1 *a mountainside.* Literally, "the mountain." It is not the topography but the theology that is important here. To the original Jewish readers, this would have been an inescapable allusion to the time long ago when Moses climbed Mt. Sinai and delivered the Law to Israel. Jesus is being portrayed as the "prophet like" Moses to whom the people are to listen (Deut. 18:15).

sat down. Typically, when rabbis taught in the synagogue, they would sit rather than stand (like modern preachers). This also accents Jesus' authoritative position.

disciples. This teaching is for everyone who would be a follower of Jesus.

5:3–10 The "Beatitudes" are so named because in the Latin translation each of the eight statements (three are in this unit and the remaining five are in the next unit) begins with the word *beatus.* Such pronouncements of blessedness were common in the Old Testament, particularly the Psalms (see Ps. 1:1; 32:1–2). Each of Jesus' beatitudes begins by defining the character (the spiritual state) of those who are members of the kingdom of God; it then moves to the reward such a person can expect. For all but the first and last beatitudes, the rewards are each expressed in the future tense. However, the Beatitudes have both a present and a future fulfillment. The Beatitudes are not defining eight different types of people but the characteristics that are to be found in every child of God. While there is a tension in this section (and throughout the Sermon) between the ideal (presented here) and the real (the presence of sin and failure), Jesus is here defining the character that is to be formed in his disciples.

5:3 *Blessed are.* The Greek word *makarios* refers to those who are to be congratulated or who are for-

tunate or well-off. It does not mean they are happy or prospering. Instead, whether or not they know or feel it, they are fortunate because their condition reflects that they are in a right relationship to God. In commenting on the meaning of this word as it is found in the beatitudes of the Psalms, Martin Buber wrote, "This is a joyful cry and an enthusiastic declaration: How fortunate indeed is this man! In the cry, timeless by its nature, the division of now and later, of earthly and future life is virtually absorbed. … The psalmist obviously wishes to say, 'Pay attention, for there is a secret good fortune … which counterbalances and outbalances all misfortune. You do not see it, but it is the true, indeed the only good fortune' " (Lapide).

poor in spirit. This phrase does not refer to those who are poor in the material sense, but to those who acknowledge their need of God. Luke's version omits the words "in spirit." Quite often, both in the Old Testament and the New Testament, the spiritually poor were literally poor as well, because their insistence on being faithful to God made them targets of oppression and exploitation by those who compromised God's standards for their own material gain. For instance, Isaiah 61:1ff, which serves as a background for the Beatitudes, announces the coming of God's deliverance to the Jewish exiles who were "lowly" (poor), "brokenhearted" (mourning), and "captives" in a hostile land (the meek). It is not an idealistic notion of the supposed simplicity of poverty, but rather a reflection of the inner character of the person who would be a follower of Jesus. "… a proper understanding of (this sermon) requires a divine transformation of the human spirit. … it cannot be read properly apart from an acknowledgment of our spiritual bankruptcy. … an acknowledgment of our poverty and of our need to be transformed is the first condition that the Sermon on the Mount imposes" (Vaught).

theirs is the kingdom of heaven. This pronouncement ushers in a new order. Traditionally, Jews assumed the reign of God meant the exaltation and leadership of Israel over all the nations. In one brief sentence, Jesus undermines such nationalistic ideas. God's kingdom, conceived of as a state of peace, fullness, justice and abundance (Isa. 42; 49; 51; 65:17–25), is promised to *anyone* recognizing his or her need for God. Whether or not one was an Israelite was simply no longer the defining issue! The Beatitudes assert that in Jesus this deliverance has come for *all* types of people who acknowledge their need and dependence upon God. Such is Jesus' message to any group who would assume that only certified members of that particular religious, racial, or ethnic group are heirs to God's kingdom.

5:4 *those who mourn.* This does not refer to those bereaved by the common tragedies that come upon all people, but to those who are in touch with the pain of the world caused by the pride, arrogance and evil of people who do not recognize their bankruptcy before God. In short, this is a mourning over sin, both that which is intensely personal and that which is broadly social. These are people who mourn over their own sin and its consequences to others. These are people who mourn over the way sin infects even the best-intentioned social, governmental and religious structures, and often leads these systems to inflict harm on multitudes of people. These are people who mourn over the pain that has come to them, because their commitment to follow the way of the kingdom of God has been met by hostility and ridicule from others. These are people who mourn over the pain that human evil brings to the whole world.

they will be comforted. "(Christian spirituality) … demands that we own our personal brokenness, especially that which occurs because of our own sin. It demands that we confess that we have betrayed our call to be faithful to God's plan. If we do not admit that sin is part of our experience and mourn over it we will be controlled by it. But, to the depth and degree that we own the brokenness in our individual lives, to the same depth and degree we will experience the blessedness of God's comfort, healing, and consolation. Only when we are willing to face our own inner alienation from God will we be able to experience the sense of wholeness that expresses messianic peace and fulfillment" (Crosby).

5:5 *the meek.* This is similar in meaning to the phrase "the poor in spirit." It involves a lifestyle marked by gentleness, humility and courteousness. The word used here for meekness is the same one used of Jesus himself in Matthew 11:28–30, in which he is called "gentle and humble in heart."

they will inherit the earth. The irony of God's reign is that, despite the efforts of those who grasp for the world, it will one day be given over to those who have demonstrated a life of meekness. This was dramatically seen in two instances in Israel's past,

e.g., in the Exodus from Egypt and, centuries later, when Israel was restored to Palestine after the Exile in Babylon. The mightiest nations on earth (first Egypt, and then Babylon) could not prevent God from accomplishing his plan for his people.

On Poverty of Spirit ...

This is not simply an internal attitude of feeling bad about myself. That is simply having low self-esteem. The attitude called for here is illustrated by Jesus' call to the rich young ruler. Only as he sold all that he had (and thus gave up the props which allowed him to maintain his illusion that he had somehow earned such blessings from God) and gave it away to help others could he be a true follower of Jesus. "The reign of God is composed of people who (sell) their power, possessions, and prestige in such a manner that they enable conditions of powerlessness, poverty, and depression in others to be alleviated" (Michael Crosby, *Spirituality of the Beatitudes,* Orbis, 1981, p. 49).

On Mourning ...

"When was the last time we really grieved over such things as the sexism in our churches, the consumerism that tears apart families, or the ideology that justifies destruction of whole peoples and the environment in the name of freedom? Healing will never come (within our society) until we first admit the existence of the sins and cultural addictions that contribute to human and societal brokenness, and then mourn over them" (Michael Crosby, *Spirituality of the Beatitudes,* Orbis, 1981, p. 90).

On Meekness ...

As can be seen from the life of Jesus, meekness means neither weakness nor timidity. Rather, it means a compassionate use of one's strengths for the good of others. Philippians 2:4–7 provides an illustration of this quality in that Jesus willingly laid aside his rights as the divine Son of God in order to give himself in service to humanity. In that letter, Paul holds out the example of Jesus as a model for all Christians to imitate. "The aggressive (people) are unable to enjoy their ill-gotten gains. Only the meek have the capacity to enjoy in life all those things that provide genuine and lasting satisfaction" (Robert Mounce, *Matthew: A Good News Commentary,* Harper and Row, 1985).

2 The Beatitudes—Matthew 5:6–12

THREE-PART AGENDA

ICE-BREAKER
15 Minutes

BIBLE STUDY
30 Minutes

CARING TIME
15–45 Minutes

LEADER: If there's a new person in your group in this session, start with an ice-breaker (see page M7 in the center section). Then begin the session with a word of prayer. If you have more than seven in your group, see the box about the "Fearless Foursome" on page 4. Count off around the group: "one, two, one, two, etc."—and have the "ones" move quickly to another room for the Bible Study.

TO BEGIN THE BIBLE STUDY TIME
(Choose 1 or 2)

1. When you're really hungry, what food do you crave the most?

2. Growing up, how did your parents make peace between you and your sibling(s)?

3. What is your typical reaction when someone cuts you off in traffic?

READ SCRIPTURE & DISCUSS
(If you don't have time for all the questions in this section, conclude the Bible Study [30 min.] by answering question #7.)

1. How was your attitude today: Great—couldn't be better? Fair—room for improvement? Poor—I don't want to talk about it?

2. On a scale of 1 (not at all) to 10 (totally) how much of a hunger and thirst for righteousness do you have right now?

The Beatitudes (continued)

> [6]"Blessed are those who hunger and thirst for
> righteousness,
> for they will be filled.
> [7]Blessed are the merciful,
> for they will be shown mercy.
> [8]Blessed are the pure in heart,
> for they will see God.
> [9]Blessed are the peacemakers,
> for they will be called sons of God.
> [10]Blessed are those who are persecuted because
> of righteousness,
> for theirs is the kingdom of heaven.

[11]"Blessed are you when people insult you, persecute you and falsely say all kinds of evil against you because of me. [12]Rejoice and be glad, because great is your reward in heaven, for in the same way they persecuted the prophets who were before you."

P.S. Add new group members to the Group Directory inside the front cover.

3. Are you better at showing mercy or receiving mercy? When has someone shown mercy to you in your life?

4. What does it mean to you to be "pure in heart"? How is that accomplished?

5. Where are you a "peacemaker": In your home? At church? At work? In your neighborhood? In what ways do you try to make peace?

6. Who is someone you admire for taking a stand in the face of adversity? How willing are you to take a stand for Christ?

7. Of the five Beatitudes in this session, which one do you most desire in your life right now?

CARING TIME
(Choose 1 or 2 of these questions before taking prayer requests and closing in prayer. Be sure to pray for the empty chair.)

1. If you had to describe this past week of your life in weather terms, what would you say: Sunny and warm? Patchy fog? Cold and rainy? Stormy? Hurricane warnings?

2. Who is someone you could invite to this group?

3. How can the group pray for you this week?

Note: The group may also want to pray for those who are being "persecuted because of righteousness."

Notes—Matthew 5:6–12

5:6 *hunger and thirst for righteousness.* Kingdom people are not to be stuck in the mourning of their sin and spiritual poverty, but are to be stirred by such insight into positive action that marks their conversion to a whole different way of life. In the ancient world, hunger and thirst were common experiences. Hungry and thirsty people have only one passion. Their entire energy is focused upon finding food and water. They will lay aside other pursuits in order to get these critical needs met. Likewise, people in Christ's kingdom are marked by this same deep-seated, intense need and longing for knowing and living in God's way (see Ps. 42:1–2; Isa. 55:1–2). Righteousness is not so much a matter of living in compliance with a set of laws as it is living in such a way that reflects the character of God in all of one's relationships. "… the desire for righteousness … means ultimately the desire to be free from sin in all its forms and in its every manifestation" (Lloyd-Jones). Stated positively, it is a desire to pursue God's will in every aspect of one's life (see also Matt. 6:33). It is the human action associated with the request in the Lord's Prayer for God's will to "be done on earth as it is in heaven."

filled. Because righteousness defines the very character of God, those who pursue it can be assured of the ultimate satisfaction of their desire when God's kingdom is manifested in all its fullness.

5:7 *the merciful.* Just as righteousness is part of the very nature of God, so is mercy. To be merciful is not a matter of having an easygoing nature that simply lets a lot of things go by, but it is an act of deliberate compassion and kindness toward those who do not deserve it. The Old Testament Law instituted mercy through the provision of the Year of Jubilee, during which all slaves were to be freed, all debts canceled, and all land returned to the original owners (Lev. 25:8–55). It is this time of restoration that was used as a picture for what "the year of the Lord's favor" (Isa. 61:2) would be like for people enslaved and/or victimized by sin. Mercy focuses upon the pain, brokenness and misery that marks the human condition as a result of sin and seeks to do what it can to relieve such conditions. Mercy gives freely to those to whom one is not expected to give at all. It offers forgiveness to those who have harmed us. It provides for the needs of those to whom we have no formal obligation. The motivation for such action stems from a person's recognition of his or her own spiritual bankruptcy; having seen the true condition of his or her own heart before God, he or she cannot help but extend mercy to others who are likewise bankrupt.

shown mercy. As the parable in Matthew 18:21–35 indicates, God's judgment of us reflects the way we treat others. This does not mean we earn God's mercy by our actions, but simply that those who refuse to show mercy betray that they have failed to recognize their own desperate need for God's mercy. In contrast, those who show mercy reveal that they recognize their own need for mercy. In this promise, Jesus assures them that they will indeed find mercy from God.

5:8 *pure in heart.* All of the Beatitudes have their roots in the ethic of the Old Testament, including this one. "In Psalm 24:3ff access to God's presence during temple worship is for (the person) who has 'clean hands and a pure heart.' These are the spiritually 'pure,' not the ritually or ceremonially clean" (Hill). In the Bible, the "heart" is a shorthand way of referring to the whole personality, including the intellect, emotions and actions. The call is for a thoroughgoing purity wherein every facet of our being is oriented toward a single-minded pursuit of God's way.

see God. In the Old Testament, this term was used to describe someone who experienced the favor of God. The single-minded will know what no one yet has known: the full presence of God (see John 1:18 and Rev. 22:4).

5:9 *peacemakers.* This beatitude calls for an active involvement in bringing about reconciliation between those in conflict, whether at the societal or personal level (see Ps. 34:14). Peacemaking is neither a matter of minimizing conflict nor of using force to suppress hostilities. True peacemaking involves seeking heart-to-heart reconciliation between people. It requires the rooting out of the causes of alienation and the disciplined practice of attitudes and actions that truly work for harmony to take their place. The price of peacemaking is perhaps most solemnly illustrated by the cross of Jesus. Peacemaking (in this case between God and humanity) sometimes requires that one willingly becomes the lightning rod, absorbing the hatred that would otherwise destroy others.

sons of God. To be called a son or a child of someone meant that a person's character was seen as a reflection of the master or teacher whom he followed. It is in this sense that those who work for peace will be acknowledged to be the children of God, since God himself is the author of peace and reconciliation.

5:10 *persecuted.* The final beatitude focuses on the persecution that comes to those who live out the ways of God. Many first-century Christians knew what it was like to be persecuted (see 1 Peter 1:6; 3:13–17; 4:12–19).

because of righteousness. This persecution comes as a result of pursuing God's way in contrast to the way of the world. The hostility Jesus encountered from the religious leaders of his time illustrates the price those who pursue God's agenda may have to pay.

kingdom of heaven. Just as this is the reward promised in the first beatitude, so it is also promised in the final beatitude. The kingdom of heaven sums up all that is involved in coming into the orbit of God and becoming part of his world.

5:11–12 This is not an additional beatitude. Rather, it is a comment on the final beatitude (v. 10). The opposition in view is that which is suffered because of one's loyalty to Jesus and his kingdom. Three types of opposition are noted: insults, persecution and lies.

5:12 *be glad.* This is literally, "to leap exceedingly." The response of the Christian to this type of mistreatment is to be that of unrestrained joy. This is not because of a "persecution complex" that derives joy out of opposition, but out of a recognition that such mistreatment at the hands of the world is an indication that one is faithful to God.

reward in heaven. In order to avoid misusing the name of the Lord (and thus violating the third commandment—Ex. 20:7), Jews commonly used the word "heaven" as a synonym for "God." Matthew follows this custom. This promise is not so much looking to a heavenly afterlife, but simply asserting that such people have a rich reward with God.

the prophets. According to Jewish tradition, Isaiah was sawn in two by those refusing to hear his prophecy; Jeremiah was stoned by his own people;

Ezekiel was ridiculed; Amos was told to leave and prophesy somewhere else (Amos 7:10–13). Moses, Samuel, Elijah and Elisha likewise met with opposition. John the Baptist was beheaded. Jesus would be crucified. The person who maintains loyalty to God needs to be reminded of the ultimate end awaiting him or her, because the possibility of opposition in this life is exceedingly high.

On Hungering and Thirsting ...

The seeking of righteousness impacts our business, political and social life every bit as much as it does our personal relationships. The call is to pursue God's agenda in *all* our dealings. "For biblical righteousness is more than a private and personal affair; it includes social righteousness as well ... liberation from oppression ... the promotion of civil rights, justice in the law courts, integrity in business dealings and honor in home and family affairs" (John R.W. Stott, *The Message of the Sermon on the Mount,* InterVarsity, 1978).

On Seeing God ...

"In a sense there is a vision of God even while we are in this world. Christian people can see God in nature ... the Christian sees God in the events of history. ... But there is a seeing also in the sense of knowing Him, a sense of feeling He is near, and enjoying His presence.

"But of course that is a mere nothing as compared with what is yet to be. ... You and I are meant for the audience chamber of God; you and I are being prepared to enter into the presence of the King of kings" (D. Martyn Lloyd-Jones, *Studies on the Sermon on the Mount,* Vol. 2, Eerdmans, 1960, p. 114).

On Being Persecuted for Righteousness ...

"Blessed are those who die for reasons that are real, for they themselves are real.

"Blessed are all those who yet can sing when all the theater is empty and the orchestra is gone.

"Blessed is the man who stands before the cruelest king and only fears his God" (Calvin Miller, *The Singer,* InterVarsity, 1975, pp. 70–71).

3 Salt & Light—Matthew 5:13–20

THREE-PART AGENDA

ICE-BREAKER
15 Minutes

BIBLE STUDY
30 Minutes

CARING TIME
15–45 Minutes

> *LEADER: Remember to choose an appropriate ice-breaker if you have a new person at the meeting (see page M7 in the center section), and then begin with a prayer. If you have more than seven in your group, divide into groups of four for the Bible Study (see the box about the "Fearless Foursome" on page 4).*

TO BEGIN THE BIBLE STUDY TIME
(Choose 1 or 2)

1. How much salt do you use to season your food?

2. What's the most spectacular display of lights you've ever seen?

3. As a teenager, what rule (Thou Shalt Not ...) was the "law of the land" in your house? What were the consequences for breaking "the law"?

READ SCRIPTURE & DISCUSS
(If you don't have time for all the questions in this section, conclude the Bible Study [30 min.] by answering question #7.)

1. If you were to describe yourself as a flavor (salt, sugar, tabasco, etc.), what would it be and why?

2. How much influence does the Christian community have on things in your city?

3. What does it mean for followers of Christ to be salt? What is one way you try to be salt and light?

Salt and Light

[13]*"You are the salt of the earth. But if the salt loses its saltiness, how can it be made salty again? It is no longer good for anything, except to be thrown out and trampled by men.*

[14]*"You are the light of the world. A city on a hill cannot be hidden.* [15]*Neither do people light a lamp and put it under a bowl. Instead they put it on its stand, and it gives light to everyone in the house.* [16]*In the same way, let your light shine before men, that they may see your good deeds and praise your Father in heaven.*

The Fulfillment of the Law

[17]*"Do not think that I have come to abolish the Law or the Prophets; I have not come to abolish them but to fulfill them.* [18]*I tell you the truth, until heaven and earth disappear, not the smallest letter, not the least stroke of a pen, will by any means disappear from the Law until everything is accomplished.* [19]*Anyone who breaks one of the least of these commandments and teaches others to do the same will be called least in the kingdom of heaven, but whoever practices and teaches these commands will be called great in the kingdom of heaven.* [20]*For I tell you that unless your righteousness surpasses that of the Pharisees and the teachers of the law, you will certainly not enter the kingdom of heaven."*

4. What did Jesus mean by saying he came to fulfill the Law and the Prophets (see notes on v. 17)?

5. How do we obtain a righteousness that surpasses that of the Pharisees?

6. This past week, how bright did your light shine: As a flickering candle? A steady campfire? A blazing furnace? How can you add fuel to the fire?

7. What practical way can this group be salt and light this week? What way can you be salt and light?

CARING TIME
(Choose 1 or 2 of these questions before taking prayer requests and closing in prayer. Be sure to pray for the empty chair.)

1. Does your group have a person for every position on the team roster (see page M5 in the center section)?

2. In what area of your life do you feel particularly challenged to "let your light shine"?

3. How can this group pray for you?

5:13–16 Matthew follows up the Beatitudes with Jesus' declaration that the children of God (whom he has just described) ought to bring these qualities to the world around them. While the final beatitude described the reaction of the world to the members of the kingdom of God, these verses point out the role the members of the kingdom play in the world. While persecution may be what is in store for the believer, "aloofness or isolationism" (Hendriksen) is simply not an option for the Christian community. Instead, Christians are to be like salt (which preserves and flavors) and light (which gives illumination and insight) to the very world that so often opposes them. The Christian faith is not a pious retreat from the realities of life. Rather, it is a call to press the values of the kingdom (as reflected in the Beatitudes) into all of life's affairs.

5:13 *salt.* Salt was a basic commodity in the ancient world. It was used to season, preserve and purify food. In the days before refrigeration, meat could be preserved indefinitely if properly salted and cured. In like manner, the children of God are to flavor the world around them with God's ways and to prevent it from going rancid. Like salt, which does its work quietly and mysteriously, so Christians are to be God's agents who combat decay and evil in the world.

loses its saltiness. Pure salt does not lose its taste. However, "what was the popularly called 'salt' was in fact a white powder (perhaps from around the Dead Sea) which, while containing sodium chloride (the chemicals which make up true salt), also contained much else since … there were no refineries. Of this dust the sodium chloride was probably the most soluble component and so the most easily washed out. The residue of white powder still looked like salt, and was doubtless still called salt, but it neither tasted nor acted like salt. It was just road dust" (Stott).

trampled. The saltless white powder was used as a surfacing material for roads. If Jesus' followers lose their distinctive character (that is, if they fail to press after the qualities reflected in the Beatitudes), they will become useless to the world. " 'What a downcome,' comments A.B. Bruce, 'from being saviours of society to supplying materials for footpaths!' " (Stott).

5:14 *light.* Light is another basic element of life. The function of light is to illuminate, to drive the darkness away. It is often used throughout the Bible as a description for God, the Messiah, or the nation of Israel (Isa. 42:6; 49:6; John 1:9; 8:12; 9:5; 1 John 1:5). Here, it is used to describe the effect on the world of those who embrace the values of the kingdom of God. Such people will illuminate the world's darkness, bringing it light and life.

of the world. Just as Israel's original purpose was to be a nation that so reflected God's nature that the Gentile nations would be drawn to its light (Isa. 49:6), so the church is to be a community whose lifestyle draws others to God. The concern of Jesus, as expressed in this saying, is not simply for one nation or type of people but for the whole world.

5:14b–15 The very purpose of light is defeated if it is hidden away. It is meant to be out in the open. Just as a city situated upon a hill cannot be hid from view, no one would think of lighting a lamp only to hide it under a bowl.

the house. Houses were typically simple one-room structures. A candle or lamp lit in any part of such a house would obviously shed light throughout the whole structure. In the same way, the character of those people who embrace God's kingdom will stand out like a light that radiates its energy throughout the whole world. Jesus' disciples are not to be secret about their discipleship, but are to live openly so that others can see who and what they are.

5:16 *let your light shine before men.* What constitutes the "light" of Christians is what they say and do.

praise your Father. While the eighth beatitude pointed out that persecution is one response the world will have toward those who embody the qualities of God's kingdom, here the point is made that another response will be that some people will recognize in these qualities the character of God. Such people will be led to give praise to God and come to faith in him.

5:17–20 The Christian's relationship to the Old Testament Law was a troubling point for the early Christian communities, which were composed primarily of Jewish converts. Here, Matthew presents in general terms Jesus' relationship to the Law.

5:17 *Do not think that I have come to abolish the Law.* The charter of the kingdom, expressed in terms of its character (vv. 3–12) and mission (vv.

13–16), does not do away with the Law but brings it to life. Jesus will complete the Old Testament; he is the one to whom the Old Testament pointed; through his ministry its intent will be fulfilled.

the Law or the Prophets. "The Law" was the way the Jews referred to the first five books of the Old Testament (the Pentateuch), while "the Prophets" refer to the major and minor prophets as well as the historical books like Kings and Chronicles.

fulfill. By his teaching, Jesus seeks to give full expression to the intention of the Law. In contrast, for all their concern about the Law (and by their pre-occupation with its details), the Pharisees and other religious leaders often overlooked its purpose. This is clearly brought out in the various examples Jesus gives in 5:21–6:18.

5:18 *I tell you the truth.* Literally, this is "for truly I say to you," a phrase characteristic of Jesus. No other teacher of his era was known to say this.

the smallest letter / least stroke of a pen. Some Hebrew and Aramaic characters are distinguishable only by a small line or dot. Jesus is accenting the validity of the Law as the ethical norm of members of God's kingdom.

until everything is accomplished. This probably refers back to the phrase "until heaven and earth disappear." Until God's plan for history is complete, the ethical demands of God's Law remain in force. Jesus' mission was not to alter these demands, but to call people to embrace them in a deep, internal way that would penetrate their whole being.

5:19 Jesus accents the point. The commands of the Law are eternally valid as an expression of God's nature. Anyone who minimizes them betrays his or her own lack of understanding about the nature of the kingdom.

5:20 *the Pharisees and the teachers of the law.* To stress the point even further, the lifestyle of the members of God's kingdom is contrasted to that of the people who were considered to be the most religious in Israel. This statement by Jesus must have shocked the disciples. If the standards of the scribes and Pharisees were not high enough to enter the kingdom, what possible hope could they have of meeting even more demanding standards?

As the following six antitheses (5:21–48) show, Jesus' conception of righteousness is not a matter of conforming to even more rules, but of stripping away external regulations altogether to focus on what is going on in one's heart.

Salt and Light

"The salt and light metaphors which Jesus used have much to teach us about our Christian responsibilities in the world.

a. *There is a fundamental difference between ... the church and the world.* We serve neither God, nor ourselves, nor the world by attempting to obliterate or even minimize this difference. ... Probably the greatest tragedy of the church throughout its ... history has been its constant tendency to conform to the prevailing culture instead of developing a Christian counterculture.

b. *We must accept the responsibility which this distinction puts upon us.* ... The function of salt is largely negative: it prevents decay. The function of light is positive: it illumines the darkness.

"... God intends us to penetrate the world. Christian salt has no business to remain snugly in elegant little ecclesiastical salt cellars; our place is to be rubbed into the secular community, as salt is rubbed into meat, to stop it going bad. ...

"... Christian people should be more outspoken in condemning evil ... and alongside this condemnation of what is false and evil, we should take our stand boldly for what is true, good, and decent. ... To try to improve society is not worldliness but love. To wash your hands of society is not love but worldliness.

"But fallen human beings need more than barricades to stop them becoming as bad as they could be. They need regeneration, new life through the gospel. Hence our second vocation to be 'the light of the world.' ... We are called both to spread the gospel and to frame our manner of life in a way that is worthy of the gospel.

"So then we should never put our two vocations to be salt and light, our Christian social and evangelistic responsibilities, over against each other as if we had to choose between them. ... The world needs both. It is bad and needs salt; it is dark and needs light. Our Christian vocation is to be both" (John R.W. Stott, *The Message of the Sermon on the Mount,* InterVarsity Press,1978, pp. 66–67).

4 Anger With a Brother—Matt. 5:21–26

THREE-PART AGENDA

ICE-BREAKER
15 Minutes

BIBLE STUDY
30 Minutes

CARING TIME
15–45 Minutes

> **LEADER:** *If there's a new person in this session, start with an ice-breaker from the center section (see page M7). Remember to stick closely to the three-part agenda and the time allowed for each segment. Is your group praying for the empty chair?*

TO BEGIN THE BIBLE STUDY TIME
(Choose 1 or 2)

1. What's your biggest pet peeve—the thing that really gets your goat?

2. What legal case has especially caught your attention? How did you feel about the outcome?

3. Would you rather be a lawyer, judge or juror and why?

READ SCRIPTURE & DISCUSS
(If you don't have time for all the questions in this section, conclude the Bible Study [30 min.] by answering question #7.)

Starting with this passage, Jesus makes the first of several contrasts between God's standards and what the Pharisees taught.

1. How can someone tell when you're angry?

2. What's the best advice you've been given on how to deal with anger?

3. In what ways are anger and murder connected? What new standard of right and wrong is Jesus creating?

Murder

²¹ *"You have heard that it was said to the people long ago, 'Do not murder,ᵃ and anyone who murders will be subject to judgment.' ²²But I tell you that anyone who is angry with his brotherᵇ will be subject to judgment. Again, anyone who says to his brother, 'Raca,ᶜ' is answerable to the Sanhedrin. But anyone who says, 'You fool!' will be in danger of the fire of hell.*

²³ *"Therefore, if you are offering your gift at the altar and there remember that your brother has something against you, ²⁴leave your gift there in front of the altar. First go and be reconciled to your brother; then come and offer your gift.*

²⁵ *"Settle matters quickly with your adversary who is taking you to court. Do it while you are still with him on the way, or he may hand you over to the judge, and the judge may hand you over to the officer, and you may be thrown into prison. ²⁶I tell you the truth, you will not get out until you have paid the last penny.ᵈ"*

ᵃ21 Exodus 20:13   ᵇ22 Some manuscripts *brother without cause*
ᶜ22 An Aramaic term of contempt   ᵈ26 Greek *kodrantes*

4. What would Jesus say about our quick-to-sue society? How literally should we take his comments about settling out of court?

5. Jesus uses the word "brother" four times in verses 21–24. Why is he so concerned about how his followers relate to each other and reconcile conflict?

6. What's the angriest you have been lately? How did that affect you and those around you?

7. When it comes to making things right with others who comes to mind? What steps could you take this week to reconcile with that person?

CARING TIME

(Choose 1 or 2 of these questions before taking prayer requests and closing in prayer. Be sure to pray for the empty chair.)

1. How are you doing at inviting others to this group?

2. Is there an area in your life you would like this group to hold you accountable?

3. How can the group pray for you this week?

Summary. Jesus' startling statement in verse 20 sets the stage for this and the following five sections (5:27–30,31–32,33–37,38–42 and 43–48), in which he illustrates the nature of the righteousness that surpasses that of the scribes and Pharisees. These sections are known as the six antitheses, so called because each begins with the formula "You have heard … " followed by "But I tell you … ." In each case, Jesus forces his audience to consider the real meaning of the Law. While verses 17–20 emphasized Jesus' continuity with the Law, this formula emphasizes his discontinuity with its interpretation. Actually, the term "antithesis" is a bit misleading, since Jesus is not contradicting all of these statements. He does not say that while the Law prohibited murder, now it is all right to kill anyone who bothers you, nor does he say that while adultery used to be wrong, now it is all right to indulge one's sexual fantasies without limit! Lapide suggests that they should thus be considered *supertheses* rather than antitheses, since Jesus is intensifying the meaning of the Law. In this particular section, Jesus addresses the meaning of the commandment not to murder. While the scribes had reduced the meaning of this command to simply a prohibition of the actual act, Jesus reveals that its intent is to expose the murderous desires that are found in instances of anger, insult, ridicule and conflict. To accent its meaning, he offers three examples of murderous relationships (5:22) followed by two illustrations meant to encourage the active pursuit of reconciliation (5:23–26).

5:21–22 The sixth commandment says "Do not murder" (Ex. 20:13), but Jesus focuses on the inner attitudes that give rise to murder (such as anger, contempt and slander). To accent the penalty associated with such attitudes, two contrasts are offered: (1) Those who actually commit murder are subject to judgment at a local court (v. 21), while those who nurse anger are subject to the judgment of God (v. 22a); (2) Those who outwardly defame others are subject to the judgment of the Sanhedrin (v. 22b), while those who inwardly repudiate others are subject to the judgment of hell (v. 22c).

You have heard / but I tell you. This phrase has parallels in the Talmudic writings of the rabbis. It was used when rabbis wanted to emphasize an element of interpretation related to the Law which had been neglected or overlooked by contemporary thought. In this way, the unfolding implications of the Law could be related to the ever-changing social, political and cultural situations of the Jewish people. In these passages, Jesus draws out the depth of meaning behind certain laws.

5:22 angry. The Greek word used here describes deep-seated, smoldering, inner anger (rather than a flash of anger).

Raca. An Aramaic term of contempt: "You good-for-nothing" (Good News Bible). Since the word is simply a transliteration of the sound made in the throat of someone preparing to spit, it carries the connotation of the offensive act of spitting in another's face.

the Sanhedrin. Even though Palestine was dominated by Roman authority at this time, the Sanhedrin (a group of 70 Jewish men), was the official ruling body of the Jews. Composed of the current high priest (as well as other high priests who had been demoted from that office by Rome), members of privileged families, family heads of various traditional tribes, Pharisees, Sadducees, and scribes, this body was responsible for administering justice in matters related to Jewish law. If witnesses were present when a person acted in such a contemptible way, the person saying (or doing) such things was subject to discipline by the Sanhedrin.

You fool! This is to demean another person's basic character. In biblical usage, to call someone a fool was to accuse him or her of being morally deficient. Since the Greek word for fool sounds very similar to that of the Hebrew word for rebel, it may be that the person is actually accused of being apostate from God. In either case, the point is that the person is viewed as being worthless, thus providing the speaker with some type of internal justification for his or her mistreatment of the person.

hell. Literally, this is Gehenna, a ravine outside Jerusalem where, in ancient times, children were once sacrificed to the god Molech (1 Kings 11:7). Because of such activity, the Jews considered it a defiled place. Their only use for it was as a garbage dump which was continually burning. Gehenna became a symbol for extreme horror, the place of punishment and spiritual death. The person who allows anger to smolder within is in danger of being consumed by smoldering fires.

5:23–26 Instead of cultivating the attitudes that might lead to the actual committing of murder, members of God's kingdom are to place the highest priority upon reconciliation with one another. Verses 23–24 underscore the point that this takes precedence over acts of worship, while verses 25–26 use an illustration from the legal situation of the day to make the point.

5:23 *altar.* The picture is of someone going to worship at the temple in Jerusalem, the only site where sacrifices could be offered. The gift the person is taking probably would have been an animal for sacrifice.

your brother. Four times the word brother is used (vv. 22–24). These principles are not so much aimed at relationships in the world, but at those within the community of the church itself. It is by practicing these principles that the church shows itself to be a radically different community from the ones found in the world.

has something against you. The responsibility for initiating reconciliation lies with the one who, whether on purpose or by accident, has offended another member of the community.

5:24 Much of the Old Testament Law dealt with matters of ceremonial worship. Proper observance of the worship traditions and regulations was very important to the Jews. While Jesus did not deny the importance of worship, his stress here is that pursuing reconciliation with someone whom one has offended takes precedence even over acts related to worship. One was not to approach God while neglecting to directly address the sin committed against another person. This was not a new emphasis. Isaiah the prophet warned the people that unless they pursued justice with one another their acts of worship were abominations in God's eyes (Isa. 1:10–17). However, in Jesus' day, popular spirituality had once again been reduced to ceremonial and legal observance of the traditions.

5:25–26 The second illustration of the importance of reconciliation is drawn from the legal system, in which a person is being taken to court over a dispute. Rather than aggravating the situation (by allowing it to fester until a judge has to determine one's guilt and prescribe punishment), it would be far better to acknowledge one's wrongdoing and seek to make amends so that court action is dropped. The basic principle in both illustrations is that when we become aware that we have offended someone, we should take immediate action to seek reconciliation and restore peace.

5:25 *court.* The Jews were offended by the Gentile custom of having debtors thrown in jail, where it was impossible for them to earn money and so pay off their debt. Yet this is the image Jesus uses to describe the situation before God of the person who refuses to seek reconciliation.

5:26 *penny.* The smallest Roman coin.

Interpreting the Law

It is popularly thought that the six antitheses in Matthew 5 are meant to show that Jesus was somehow doing away with the Old Testament, as though he was saying, "While the Old Testament Law says this, I say … ." This approach misses the point of Jesus' ministry and contradicts the strong statements recorded in 5:17–20. There is not an opposition here between the Law and the Gospel, Christ and Moses, or the Old Testament and the New. Rather, as John Stott notes, the contrast is between Christ's interpretation of the Law and the scribal misinterpretations.

"What … were the scribes and Pharisees doing? … In general, they were trying to reduce the challenge of the law, to 'relax' (v. 19) the commandments of God, and so make his moral demands more manageable and less exacting … .

"What the scribes and Pharisees were doing, in order to make obedience more readily attainable, was to restrict the commandments and extend the permissions of the law. They made the law's demand less demanding and the law's permissions more permissive. What Jesus did was to reverse both tendencies. He insisted instead that the full implications of God's commandments must be accepted without imposing any artificial limits, whereas the limits which God had set to his permissions must also be accepted and not arbitrarily increased.

"What Jesus did was … to explain the true meaning of the law with all its uncomfortable implications. … And in this matter Christian disciples must follow Christ, and not the Pharisees. We have no liberty to try to lower the law's standards and make it easier to obey. That is the casuistry of Pharisees, not Christians. Christian righteousness must exceed pharisaic righteousness" (John R.W. Stott, *The Message of the Sermon on the Mount,* InterVarsity Press, 1978, pp. 78–80).

5 Adultery ... Oaths—Matt. 5:27–37

THREE-PART AGENDA

ICE-BREAKER
15 Minutes

BIBLE STUDY
30 Minutes

CARING TIME
15–45 Minutes

> **LEADER:** Check page M7 in the center section for a good ice-breaker, particularly if you have a new person at this meeting. Is your group working well together—with everyone "fielding their position" as shown on the team roster on page M5?

TO BEGIN THE BIBLE STUDY TIME
(Choose 1 or 2)

1. Who was the first person you had a "crush" on—a case of puppy love?

2. What is the worst injury you had as a child?

3. What promise from God, or an individual, do you hold onto with all your might?

READ SCRIPTURE & DISCUSS
(If you don't have time for all the questions in this section, conclude the Bible Study [30 min.] by answering question #7.)

1. When it comes to "entertainment" where do you draw the line: G-rated? PG? R? Other? Where would Jesus draw the line?

2. What's the difference between being friendly, flirting, and committing adultery in the heart? What do you do to keep your thought life pure?

3. How do you feel about verses 29 and 30—what point is Jesus making (see notes on these verses)?

Adultery

[27] "You have heard that it was said, 'Do not commit adultery.'[a] [28] But I tell you that anyone who looks at a woman lustfully has already committed adultery with her in his heart. [29] If your right eye causes you to sin, gouge it out and throw it away. It is better for you to lose one part of your body than for your whole body to be thrown into hell. [30] And if your right hand causes you to sin, cut it off and throw it away. It is better for you to lose one part of your body than for your whole body to go into hell.

Divorce

[31] "It has been said, 'Anyone who divorces his wife must give her a certificate of divorce.'[b] [32] But I tell you that anyone who divorces his wife, except for marital unfaithfulness, causes her to become an adulteress, and anyone who marries the divorced woman commits adultery.

Oaths

[33] "Again, you have heard that it was said to the people long ago, 'Do not break your oath, but keep the oaths you have made to the Lord.' [34] But I tell you, Do not swear at all: either by heaven, for it is God's throne; [35] or by the earth, for it is his footstool; or by Jerusalem, for it is the city of the Great King. [36] And do not swear by your head, for you cannot make even one hair white or black. [37] Simply let your 'Yes' be 'Yes,' and your 'No,' 'No'; anything beyond this comes from the evil one."

[a]27 Exodus 20:14   [b]31 Deut. 24:1

4. How has divorce touched your life or your family? (For more on divorce, see "The Difficult Subject of Divorce" at the end of the notes.)

5. What is the heart of the matter regarding oaths (see note on v. 34)? Why is keeping promises so important?

6. What letter grade would you get for keeping promises to God? To your family? To your friends? To yourself?

7. Which of these moral demands—controlling lust, honoring marriage, keeping your word—challenges you the most?

CARING TIME

(Choose 1 or 2 of these questions before taking prayer requests and closing in prayer. Be sure to pray for the empty chair.)

1. Are all the players on the team roster fulfilling all of the assignments of their position? (Look at the roster again on page M5 of the center section.)

2. On a scale of 1 (baby steps) to 10 (giant leaps), how has your relationship with God progressed compared to where it was one year ago?

3. How can the group pray for you this week?

5:27–30 Having shown the depth of meaning behind the Law's prohibition against murder (the sixth commandment), Jesus now does the same with the seventh commandment (Ex. 20:14).

5:27 *Do not commit adultery.* While adultery is defined as having sexual relationships with another person's spouse, the Old Testament Law also prohibited fornication, incest, bestiality, homosexuality and rape. The prohibition against adultery in the Ten Commandments sums up the various prohibitions against illegitimate sexual acts.

5:28 *lustfully.* Just as anger is at the root of murder (5:21–22), so lust is at the root of adultery. "Jesus' intention is to prohibit not a natural sexual attraction, but the deliberate harboring of desire for an illicit relationship" (France).

5:29–30 In these statements Jesus is, of course, speaking in hyperbole, deliberately overstating or dramatizing in order to make a point. However, in the early part of the third century, Origen, a prominent theologian, took this literally and made himself a eunuch. Such actions were prohibited by the Council of Nicea in A.D. 325. The Council understood that Jesus was speaking figuratively to accent his point that radical action must be taken to root out sin in our lives.

eye / hand. The idea here is that if lust is stimulated via sight, then deal with lust by refusing to look at the person for whom one lusts. Likewise if temptation comes via touch, stop touching those whom you inwardly desire. Jesus is calling for a conscious, vigilant choice to turn away from sin and those things that draw one toward sin in order to pursue God's kingdom.

5:31–32 The third antithesis (though the formula is not exactly the same as the others) has to do with divorce. This subject follows naturally from the discussion of adultery and lust.

5:31 In first-century Judaism divorce was allowed on the basis of Deuteronomy 24:1–4, part of which is quoted here. In Deuteronomy the issue is whether a man can remarry his wife whom he divorced (Deut. 24:1–4 prohibits such remarriage). The thing to note is that in Deuteronomy the right to divorce and the right of the wife to remarry is assumed. However, nowhere in the Old Testament are the grounds for divorce stated. This was the subject of the debate in the first century: On what grounds could a husband

divorce his wife (only husbands had the right of divorce, though in certain instances a wife could require her husband to divorce her)? The stricter rabbis allowed divorce only on the basis of adultery. The more liberal teachers allowed divorce for a host of trivial reasons: e.g., if a woman spoiled her husband's dinner, or if her husband found her less attractive than someone else. To Jesus, such debate missed the point. It focused on ways a man could justify divorcing his wife, whereas Jesus' concern was with the true intention of marriage.

a certificate of divorce. In large part, the intent of the Law of Moses (see Deut. 24:1–4) was to protect a woman from capricious treatment by her husband. Thus he was required to give her a certificate of divorce, thereby verifying her release from the marriage and giving her the right to remarry without the threat of being accused of adultery.

5:32 In this verse, as he has done twice already (and will continue to do as the Sermon on the Mount unfolds), Jesus goes well beyond what the Law required: anger is a form of murder (5:21–26); lust is a form of adultery (5:27–30); and here, remarriage is a form of adultery. In each instance (murder, adultery, divorce), the question must be asked: who can live up to such high standards? (The disciples realize this in Matt. 19:10, where Jesus repeats his words about divorce, and respond with amazement, "If this is the situation between a husband and wife, it is better not to marry.") But this is the point. What Jesus outlines in the Sermon on the Mount is the ideal, the goal, the standards of the kingdom. He describes what *ought* to be. There ought to be no remarriage after divorce. In fact, there ought to be no divorce (Matt. 19:3–8). But, in fact, there is divorce, just as there is anger and lust. We are called to be perfect (Matt. 5:48), but none of us is. Thus, we all need to ask for forgiveness on a daily basis (Matt. 6:12). It is important to interpret Jesus' words about divorce and remarriage in the light of the whole Sermon on the Mount. He defines the perfect standard which we must strive to keep, and yet our fallenness keeps getting in the way of achieving such a goal.

except for marital unfaithfulness. The word which is translated "marital unfaithfulness" refers to a variety of sexual behaviors: "every kind of unlawful intercourse" according to the Greek dictionary. The question is, what is intended here? The word could refer to incestuous marriages involving blood relatives. Such arrangements were allowed by Roman law and were common in the Hellenistic world of the first century. They were, however, forbidden by the Old Testament Law. Or the word could refer to adulterous relationships. The point is that divorcing an unchaste woman would not *make* her an adulteress, since she is already such, so the husband would not, in this case, be responsible for forcing her into an adulterous union (a second marriage). What is offered here is not an exception that makes divorce acceptable, only an exception to the rule that all divorce is adulterous.

causes her to become an adulteress. In traditional Judaism, a man was never guilty of adultery. He could marry other women, whether he was divorced or not (polygamy was still possible though little practiced in the first century), and he could have concubines. But a wife who had sexual relations with any other man was guilty of adultery against her husband (Guelich). But here Jesus makes the man responsible for his ex-wife's adultery (should she remarry) because he divorced her. Thus Jesus' statement is stricter than custom of the time and stricter than Deuteronomy 24:1–4 (which clearly allows for remarriage on the part of women). Once again, as in verses 22 and 28, Jesus radicalizes Old Testament laws.

5:33–37 The fourth antithesis deals with the matter of keeping one's word.

5:33 *Do not break your oath.* Jesus does not so much quote the Old Testament, as he summarizes various passages on the subject of oaths (see Ex. 20:7; Lev. 19:12; Num. 30:2; Deut. 23:21–23).

5:34 *Do not swear at all.* Jesus goes beyond the Old Testament by pointing out the problem behind the fact that a person resorts to oath-taking in order to be trusted. He identifies a series of objects that people used to swear upon. Contrary to what the rabbis taught, according to Jesus it does not matter whether you swear upon God's name (which was considered binding) or on anything else (a nonbinding oath), since all objects are God's. His point is that a person's word alone should be sufficient to guarantee the accuracy of a statement. The issue in this passage is not so much against oath-taking (Jesus did not refuse the chief priest's command to swear an oath in Matt. 26:62–64), as it is having a character that is so full of integrity that others can trust our word without having to resort to an oath.

The Difficult Subject of Divorce

Jesus' statement on divorce in 5:31–32 needs to be understood in the context of the whole Sermon. Ideally, there should be no divorce. As seen from Matthew 19 and Mark 10, divorce and remarriage is a departure from God's intention for marriage. Its presence, like the presence of anger, greed and pride, betrays a lack of inner righteousness. Jesus' words about divorce in this context are meant to reveal yet another area where the so-called "righteousness" of the Pharisees was only skin-deep. The presence of divorce and remarriage among them, like lust (5:28), was indicative of the fact that in their hearts they had failed to live by the spirit of the command, "Thou shall not commit adultery."

It is important to note here that while the woman is called the adulteress, the *fault* for that situation is placed upon the husband who divorced her. In that culture, a divorced woman would have little choice for survival except to marry again. Jesus is not condemning her because of that social reality, but he is pointing out to the men involved that their casual attitude toward marriage and divorce is not much more than a "legal" way of indulging in the immorality of adultery.

To the Jews of Jesus' day, divorce and remarriage were perfectly acceptable. Neither was considered a sin. For men at least, divorce and remarriage carried no moral stigma. Jesus' statement suddenly placed their attitude toward divorce and remarriage into the category of moral evil, a reality they had never before considered. While they held that their divorces and remarriages were *legal*, Jesus asserted that they were not *moral*. Their actions betrayed inner attitudes that fell far short of the quality of love for which God looks in truly "righteous" people.

Jesus' intent in the entire Sermon is to demonstrate people's desperate need for grace. He is not running a campaign in which he is cataloging areas where new laws are needed, but is instead showing his disciples common examples from life which betrayed their lack of true, inner righteousness. His listeners then, as his readers now, were all touched in some way by anger, hate, an unforgiving spirit, lust, divorce, lack of integrity, lack of generosity, and so forth. His point is that these common realities are symptoms of our brokenness and need for grace. They are symptoms that we do not have it in ourselves to be righteous enough for God, no matter how clever we may be in devising justifications for these attitudes and actions.

6 An Eye for An Eye—Matt. 5:38–48

THREE-PART AGENDA

ICE-BREAKER
15 Minutes

BIBLE STUDY
30 Minutes

CARING TIME
15–45 Minutes

LEADER: If there's a new person in this session, start with an ice-breaker from the center section (see page M7). Remember to stick closely to the three-part agenda and the time allowed for each segment. Is your group praying for the empty chair?

TO BEGIN THE BIBLE STUDY TIME
(Choose 1 or 2)

1. In high school, who was your school's biggest rival?

2. When a panhandler asks you for money, what is your usual response?

3. What is the worst practical joke someone played on you? How did you "get even"?

READ SCRIPTURE & DISCUSS
(If you don't have time for all the questions in this section, conclude the Bible Study [30 min.] by answering question #7.)

1. Regarding crime and punishment, which statement most accurately reflects your view: Lock 'em up and throw away the key? Rehabilitation is the key? The punishment should fit the crime? Three strikes and you're out?

2. What kind of person do you have the hardest time loving?

3. What was Jesus' intent in saying, "Do not resist an evil person" (see note on v. 39)?

An Eye for an Eye

38"You have heard that it was said, 'Eye for eye, and tooth for tooth.'a 39But I tell you, Do not resist an evil person. If someone strikes you on the right cheek, turn to him the other also. 40And if someone wants to sue you and take your tunic, let him have your cloak as well. 41If someone forces you to go one mile, go with him two miles. 42Give to the one who asks you, and do not turn away from the one who wants to borrow from you.

Love for Enemies

43"You have heard that it was said, 'Love your neighborb and hate your enemy.' 44But I tell you: Love your enemiesc and pray for those who persecute you, 45that you may be sons of your Father in heaven. He causes his sun to rise on the evil and the good, and sends rain on the righteous and the unrighteous. 46If you love those who love you, what reward will you get? Are not even the tax collectors doing that? 47And if you greet only your brothers, what are you doing more than others? Do not even pagans do that? 48Be perfect, therefore, as your heavenly Father is perfect."

a38 Exodus 21:24; Lev. 24:20; Deut. 19:21   b43 Lev. 19:18
c44 Some late manuscripts *enemies, bless those who curse you, do good to those who hate you*

4. What characteristic is to distinguish a Christian from a pagan? What actions demonstrate this characteristic?

5. What is your initial reaction to verse 48? What challenge is Jesus presenting to you?

6. Since turning your life over to God, what effect has this had on your ability to love others—even those who hurt you?

7. How do you plan to respond to the radical demands of this passage?

CARING TIME

(Choose 1 or 2 of these questions before taking prayer requests and closing in prayer. Be sure to pray for the empty chair.)

1. What do you look forward to the most about these meetings?

2. What is something you feel God is challenging you to do?

3. How can the group pray for you this week?

5:38–42 The fifth antithesis has to do with revenge.

5:38 *"Eye for eye."* This is said to be the oldest law in the world. It is found in the codes of Hammurabi, a king who lived in the eighteenth century B.C., as well as three times in the Old Testament (Ex. 21:23–24; Lev. 24:20; Deut. 19:21). The law's original context was in terms of judicial punishments. Its point was usually not to *require* "eye for eye, and tooth for tooth," but to limit punishment to the extent of the crime. Without this law, the tendency among tribal people would be for an aggrieved person to seek revenge upon his or her attacker by killing that person and, perhaps, his or her entire family! Even during the time of the establishment of the Jews as a nation, this law was not literally applied. Typically, instead of strict physical punishments, monetary reimbursements were made for offenses. Thus, by Jesus' day, no Jewish court of law literally applied this principle. However, the scribes had interpreted this judicial principle into a justification for acts of personal revenge, even though such acts were explicitly prohibited by the Law (Lev. 19:18)! The scribes had transformed this law that set limits on judicial actions into an individual's right to carry out revenge in one's private affairs. Thus, it appeared that one could seek to do harm to another person and still be a good follower of God's Law!

5:39 *Do not resist an evil person.* Jesus dismisses this misinterpretation of the scribes and calls instead for an attitude of nonretaliation. In this context, "to resist" means to oppose or fight back, or to seek revenge against someone who has harmed. Love, as illustrated by Jesus' response to the abuse of the Roman guards (Matt. 27:27–31), absorbs and diffuses hate: It does not respond in kind (Rom. 12:19–21). Jesus' teaching here does not invalidate judicial practices that seek justice for crimes. The point is that injustice and evil are to be dealt with through the proper channels, and not made into personal vendettas. Nor does Jesus' teaching imply that one should never take measures to protect oneself or someone else who is being assaulted. What is prohibited is the seeking of revenge, the desire and action to harm another in order to get back at them for a wrong done against you. What is exposed is the pharisaic hypocrisy of using the Law to justify attitudes and actions the Law actually prohibited.

strikes you on the right cheek. This is the first of three examples of the principle of nonretaliation in action. "The Greek verb *rhapizo* refers to striking

another on the face with the back of the hand, an action which was regarded as a very great insult meriting punishment" (Hill). What seems to be in view here is actually more of a form of insult rather than an act of physical violence. It is the sort of thing a Roman soldier might do to a Jewish subject (or a master to a slave) to indicate his superior position.

the other also. Instead of retaliating or seeking action at the law court, this saying amounts to allowing the person to insult you again. The point is not that the believers are too weak or timid to fight back, but that they are so disciplined by love that they simply refuse to act in a way that fails to express love.

5:40 The second illustration comes from the law court. Rather than fighting your opponent in court, give what is sought; in fact, give even more than what is asked! The root idea here is not so much the avoidance of litigation as it is the encouragement to act with a generous, loving attitude toward all people.

tunic. This was the close fitting under-robe made of cotton or linen.

cloak. The Law (Ex. 22:25–26; Deut. 24:10–13) prohibited a person from seizing a person's cloak as the payment of a debt, since this woolen outer robe was used as a blanket at night. Jesus' call here is for his followers to give beyond what even the Law could require.

5:41 *forces you to go one mile.* Roman soldiers had the right to press civilians into service to carry their gear for a distance up to one mile (the Roman "mile" was 1,000 paces). The word used here is a technical term for such compulsory conscription.

5:42 This example is drawn from the practice of lending and borrowing. The follower of Jesus is to lend to those in need regardless of their perceived ability to repay. However, as in other verses in this section, a literal application of these words in every situation is probably not in view (see 5:29–30), otherwise all those in the church would soon be reduced to total poverty and would themselves be in need of constant assistance. The aim here is to encourage a free spirit of generosity (as opposed to a narrow assessment of personal gain).

5:43–48 The sixth and final antithesis has to do with the extent of love.

Leadership Training Supplement

YOU ARE HERE

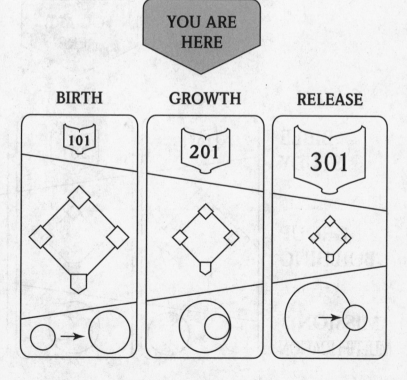

| BIRTH | GROWTH | RELEASE |
| 101 | 201 | 301 |

What is the game plan for your group in the 201 stage?

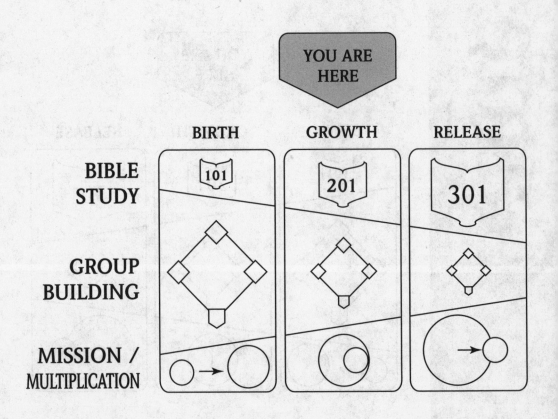

YOU ARE HERE

	BIRTH	GROWTH	RELEASE
BIBLE STUDY	101	201	301
GROUP BUILDING			
MISSION / MULTIPLICATION			

The 3-Legged Stool

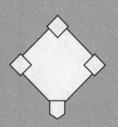

The three essentials in a healthy small group are Bible Study, Group Building and Mission / Multiplication. You need all three to stay balanced—like a 3-legged stool.
- To focus only on Bible Study will lead to scholasticism.
- To focus only on Group Building will lead to narcissism.
- To focus only on Mission will lead to burnout.

You need a game plan for the life cycle of the group where all of these elements are present in a purpose-driven strategy:

Bible Study

To dig into Scripture as a group.

Group Bible Study is quite different from individual Bible Study. The guided discussion questions are open-ended. And for those with little Bible background, there are reference notes to bring this person up to speed.

Group Building

To transform your group into a mission-driven team.

The nine basic needs of a group will be assigned to nine different people. Everyone has a job to fill, and when everyone is doing their job the group will grow spiritually and numerically. When new people enter the group, there is a selection of ICE-BREAKERS to start off the meeting and let the new people get acquainted.

Mission / Multiplication

To identify the Apprentice / Leader for birthing a new group.

In this stage, you will start dreaming about the possibility of starting a new group down the road. The questions at the close of each session will lead you carefully through the dreaming process—to help you discover an Apprentice / Leader who will eventually be the leader of a new group. This is an exciting challenge! (See page M6 for more about Mission / Multiplication.)

Bible Study

What is unique about Serendipity Group Bible Study?

Bible Study for groups is based on six principles. Principle 1: Level the playing field so that everyone can share—those who know the Bible and those who do not know the Bible. Principle 2: Share your spiritual story and let the people in your group get to know you. Principle 3: Ask open-ended questions that have no right or wrong answers. Principle 4: Keep a tight agenda. Principle 5: Subdivide into smaller groups so that everyone can participate. Principle 6: Affirm One Another—"Thanks for sharing."

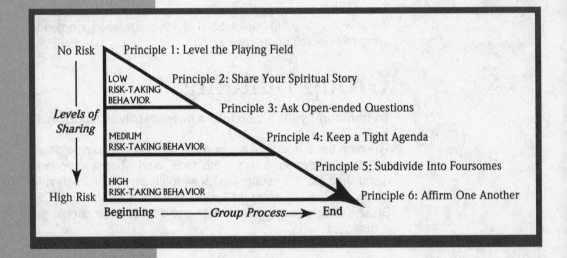

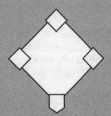

Group Building

What are the jobs that are needed on your team roster?

In the first or second session of this course, you need to fill out the roster on the next page. Then check every few weeks to see that everyone is "playing their position." If you do not have nine people in your group, you can double up on jobs until new people join your group and are assigned a job.

Your Small Group Team Roster

Mission Leader
(Left Field)
Keeps group focused on the mission to invite new people and eventually give birth to a new group. This person needs to be passionate and have a long-term perspective.

_____

Host
(Center Field)
Environmental engineer in charge of meeting location. Always on the lookout for moving to a new meeting location where new people will feel the "home field advantage."

_____

Social Leader
(Right Field)
Designates who is going to bring refreshments. Plans a party every month or so where new people are invited to visit and children are welcome.

_____

Caretaker
(Shortstop)
Takes new members under their wing. Makes sure they get acquainted. Always has an extra book, name tags and a list of group members and phone numbers.

_____

Bible Study Leader
(Second Base)
Takes over in the Bible Study time (30 minutes). Follows the agenda. Keeps the group moving. This person must be very time-conscious.

_____

Group Leader
(Pitcher)
Puts ball in play. Team encourager. Motivator. Sees to it that everyone is involved in the team effort.

_____

Caring Time Leader
(Third Base)
Takes over in the Caring Time. Records prayer requests and follows up on any prayer needs during the week. This person is the "heart" of the group.

_____

Worship Leader
(First Base)
Starts the meeting with singing and prayer. If a new person comes, shifts immediately to an ice-breaker to get acquainted, before the opening prayer.

Apprentice / Leader
(Catcher)
The other half of the battery. Observes the infield. Calls "time" to discuss strategy and regroup. Stays focused.

_____

Mission /
Multiplication

Where are you in the 3-stage life cycle of your mission?

You can't sit on a one-legged stool—or even a two-legged stool. It takes all three. The same is true of a small group; you need all three legs. A Bible Study and Care Group will eventually fall if it does not have a mission.

The mission goal is to eventually give birth to a new group. In this 201 course, the goals are: 1) to keep inviting new people to join your group and 2) to discover the Apprentice / Leader and leadership core for starting a new group down the road.

When a new person comes to the group, start off the meeting with one of the ice-breakers on the following pages. These ice-breakers are designed to be fun and easy to share, but they have a very important purpose—that is, to let the new person get acquainted with the group and share their spiritual story with the group, and hear the spiritual stories of those in the group.

YOU ARE HERE

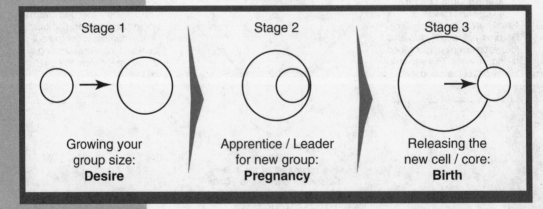

Stage 1	Stage 2	Stage 3
Growing your group size: **Desire**	Apprentice / Leader for new group: **Pregnancy**	Releasing the new cell / core: **Birth**

Ice-Breakers

I Am Somebody Who ...

Rotate around the group, one person reading the first item, the next person reading the second item, etc. Before answering, let everyone in the group try to GUESS what the answer would be: "Yes" ... "No" ... or "Maybe." After everyone has guessed, explain the answer. Anyone who guessed right gets $10. When every item on the list has been read, the person with the most "money" WINS.

I AM SOMEBODY WHO ...

Y N M
- ❒ ❒ ❒ would go on a blind date
- ❒ ❒ ❒ sings in the shower
- ❒ ❒ ❒ listens to music full blast
- ❒ ❒ ❒ likes to dance
- ❒ ❒ ❒ cries at movies
- ❒ ❒ ❒ stops to smell the flowers
- ❒ ❒ ❒ daydreams a lot
- ❒ ❒ ❒ likes to play practical jokes
- ❒ ❒ ❒ makes a "to do" list
- ❒ ❒ ❒ loves liver
- ❒ ❒ ❒ won't use a portable toilet
- ❒ ❒ ❒ likes thunderstorms
- ❒ ❒ ❒ enjoys romance novels
- ❒ ❒ ❒ loves crossword puzzles
- ❒ ❒ ❒ hates flying
- ❒ ❒ ❒ fixes my own car

Y N M
- ❒ ❒ ❒ would enjoy skydiving
- ❒ ❒ ❒ has a black belt in karate
- ❒ ❒ ❒ watches soap operas
- ❒ ❒ ❒ is afraid of the dark
- ❒ ❒ ❒ goes to bed early
- ❒ ❒ ❒ plays the guitar
- ❒ ❒ ❒ talks to plants
- ❒ ❒ ❒ will ask a stranger for directions
- ❒ ❒ ❒ sleeps until the last second
- ❒ ❒ ❒ likes to travel alone
- ❒ ❒ ❒ reads the financial page
- ❒ ❒ ❒ saves for a rainy day
- ❒ ❒ ❒ lies about my age
- ❒ ❒ ❒ yells at the umpire
- ❒ ❒ ❒ closes my eyes during scary movies

Press Conference

This is a great activity for a new group or when new people are joining an established group. Interview one person with these questions.

1. What is your nickname and how did you get it?

2. Where did you grow up? Where was the "watering hole" in your hometown—where kids got together?

3. What did you do for kicks then? What about now?

4. What was the turning point in your spiritual life?

5. What prompted you to come to this group?

6. What do you want to get out of this group?

Down Memory Lane

Celebrate the childhood memories of the way you were. Choose one or more of the topics listed below and take turns answering the question related to it. If time allows, do another round.

HOME SWEET HOME–What do you remember about your childhood home?

TELEVISION—What was your favorite TV program or radio show?

OLD SCHOOLHOUSE—What were your best and worst subjects in school?

LIBRARY—What did you like to read (and where)?

TELEPHONE—How much time did you spend on the phone each day?

MOVIES—Who was your favorite movie star?

CASH FLOW—What did you do for spending money?

SPORTS—What was your favorite sport or team?

GRANDPA'S HOUSE—Where did your grandparents live? When did you visit them?

POLICE—Did you ever get in trouble with the law?

WEEKENDS—What was the thing to do on Saturday night?

Wallet Scavenger Hunt

With your wallet or purse, use the set of questions below. You get two minutes in silence to go through your possessions and find these items. Then break the silence and "show-and-tell" what you have chosen. For instance, "The thing I have had for the longest time is ... this picture of me when I was a baby."

1. The thing I have had for the LONGEST TIME in my wallet is ...

2. The thing that has SENTIMENTAL VALUE is ...

3. The thing that reminds me of a FUN TIME is ...

4. The most REVEALING thing about me in my wallet is ...

The Grand Total

This is a fun ice-breaker that has additional uses. You can use this ice-breaker to divide your group into two subgroups (odds and evens). You can also calculate who has the highest and lowest totals if you need a fun way to select someone to do a particular task, such as bring refreshments or be first to tell their story.

Fill each box with the correct number and then total your score. When everyone is finished, go around the group and explain how you got your total.

☐	X	☐	=	☐
Number of hours you sleep		Number of miles you walk daily		Subtotal
☐	−	☐	=	☐
Number of speeding tickets you've received		Number of times sent to principal's office		Subtotal
☐	÷	☐	=	☐
Number of hours spent watching TV daily		Number of books you read this year for fun		Subtotal
☐	+	☐	=	☐
Number of push-ups you can do		Number of pounds you lost this year		Subtotal

☐

GRAND TOTAL

Find Yourself in the Picture

In this drawing, which child do you identify with—or which one best portrays you right now? Share with your group which child you would choose and why. You can also use this as an affirmation exercise, by assigning each person in your group to a child in the picture.

Four Facts, One Lie

Everyone in the group should answer the following five questions. One of the five answers should be a lie! The rest of the group members can guess which of your answers is a lie.

1. At age 7, my favorite TV show was ...

2. At age 9, my hero was ...

3. At age 11, I wanted to be a ...

4. At age 13, my favorite music was ...

5. Right now, my favorite pastime is ...

Old-Fashioned Auction

Just like an old-fashioned auction, conduct an out loud auction in your group—starting each item at $50. Everybody starts out with $1,000. Select an auctioneer. This person can also get in on the bidding. Remember, start the bidding on each item at $50. Then, write the winning bid in the left column and the winner's name in the right column. Remember, you only have $1,000 to spend for the whole game. AUCTIONEER: Start off by asking, "Who will give me $50 for a 1965 red MG convertible?" ... and keep going until you have a winner. Keep this auction to 10 minutes.

WINNING BID   WINNER

$_____ 1965 red MG convertible in perfect condition _____

$_____ Winter vacation in Hawaii for two _____

$_____ Two Super Bowl tickets on the 50-yard line _____

$_____ One year of no hassles with my kids / parents _____

$_____ Holy Land tour hosted by my favorite Christian _____
leader

$_____ Season pass to ski resort of my choice _____

$_____ Two months off to do anything I want, with pay _____

$_____ Home theater with surround sound _____

$_____ Breakfast in bed for one year _____

$_____ Two front-row tickets at the concert of my choice _____

$_____ Two-week Caribbean cruise with my spouse in _____
honeymoon suite

$_____ Shopping spree at Saks Fifth Avenue _____

$_____ Six months of maid service _____

$_____ All-expense-paid family vacation to Disney World_____

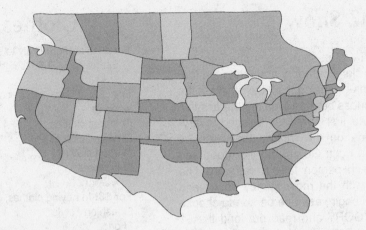

Places in My Life

On the map above, put six dots to indicate these significant places in your journey. Then go around and have each person explain the dots:

- the place where I was born
- the place where I spent most of my life
- the place where I first fell in love
- the place where I went or would like to go on a honeymoon
- the place where God first became real to me
- the place where I would like to retire

The Four Quaker Questions

This is an old Quaker activity which Serendipity has adapted over the years. Go around the group and share your answers to the questions, everyone answering #1. Then, everyone answers #2, etc. This ice-breaker has been known to take between 30 and 60 minutes for some groups.

1. Where were you living between the ages of 7 and 12, and what were the winters like then?

2. How was your home heated during that time?

3. What was the center of warmth in your life when you were a child? (It could be a place in the house, a time of year, a person, etc.)

4. When did God become a "warm" person to you ... and how did it happen?

KWIZ Show

Like a TV quiz show, someone from the group picks a category and reads the four questions—pausing to let the others in the group guess before revealing the answer. When the first person is finished, everyone adds up the money they won by guessing right. Go around the group and have each person take a category. The person with the most money at the end wins. To begin, ask one person to choose a CATEGORY and read out loud the $1 question. Before answering, let everyone try to GUESS the answer. When everyone has guessed, the person answers the question, and anyone who guessed right puts $1 in the margin, etc. until the first person has read all four questions in the CATEGORY.

Clothes

For $1: I'm more likely to shop at:
❏ Sears   ❏ Saks Fifth Avenue

For $2: I feel more comfortable wearing:
❏ formal clothes
❏ casual clothes
❏ sport clothes
❏ grubbies

For $3: In buying clothes, I look for:
❏ fashion / style
❏ price
❏ name brand
❏ quality

For $4: In buying clothes, I usually:
❏ shop all day for a bargain
❏ go to one store, but try on everything
❏ buy the first thing I try on
❏ buy without trying it on

Tastes

For $1: In music, I am closer to:
❏ Bach   ❏ Beatles

For $2: In furniture, I prefer:
❏ Early American
❏ French Provincial
❏ Scandinavian—contemporary
❏ Hodgepodge—little of everything

For $3: My favorite choice of reading material is:
❏ science fiction   ❏ sports
❏ mystery   ❏ romance

For $4: If I had $1,000 to splurge, I would buy:
❏ one original painting
❏ two numbered prints
❏ three reproductions and an easy chair
❏ four cheap imitations, an easy chair and a color TV

Travel

For $1: For travel, I prefer:
❏ excitement   ❏ enrichment

For $2: On a vacation, my lifestyle is:
❏ go-go all the time
❏ slow and easy
❏ party every night and sleep in

For $3: In packing for a trip, I include:
❏ toothbrush and change of underwear
❏ light bag and good book
❏ small suitcase and nice outfit
❏ all but the kitchen sink

For $4: If I had money to blow, I would choose:
❏ one glorious night in a luxury hotel
❏ a weekend in a nice hotel
❏ a full week in a cheap motel
❏ two weeks camping in the boondocks

Habits

For $1: I am more likely to squeeze the toothpaste:
❏ in the middle ❏ from the end

For $2: If I am lost, I will probably:
❏ stop and ask directions
❏ check the map
❏ find the way by driving around

For $3: I read the newspaper starting with the:
❏ front page
❏ funnies
❏ sports
❏ entertainment section

For $4: When I get ready for bed, I put my clothes:
❏ on a hanger in the closet
❏ folded neatly over a chair
❏ into a hamper or clothes basket
❏ on the floor

Shows

For $1: I am more likely to:
❏ go see a first-run movie
❏ rent a video at home

For $2: On TV, my first choice is:
❏ news
❏ sports
❏ sitcoms

For $3: If a show gets too scary, I will usually:
❏ go to the restroom
❏ close my eyes
❏ clutch a friend
❏ love it

For $4: In movies, I prefer:
❏ romantic comedies
❏ serious drama
❏ action films
❏ Disney animation

Food

For $1: I prefer to eat at a:
❏ fast-food restaurant
❏ fancy restaurant

For $2: On the menu, I look for something:
❏ familiar
❏ different
❏ way-out

For $3: When eating chicken, my preference is a:
❏ drumstick
❏ wing
❏ breast
❏ gizzard

For $4: I draw the line when it comes to eating:
❏ frog legs
❏ snails
❏ raw oysters
❏ Rocky Mountain oysters

Work

For $1: I prefer to work at a job that is:
❏ too big to handle
❏ too small to be challenging

For $2: The job I find most unpleasant to do is:
❏ cleaning the house
❏ working in the yard
❏ balancing the checkbook

For $3: In choosing a job, I look for:
❏ salary
❏ security
❏ fulfillment
❏ working conditions

For $4: If I had to choose between these jobs, I would choose:
❏ pickle inspector at processing plant
❏ complaint officer at department store
❏ bedpan changer at hospital
❏ personnel manager in charge of firing

Let Me Tell You About My Day

What was your day like today? Use one of the characters below to help you describe your day to the group. Feel free to elaborate.

GREEK TRAGEDY
It was classic, not a dry eye in the house.

EPISODE OF THREE STOOGES
I was Larry, trapped between Curly and Moe.

SOAP OPERA
I didn't think these things could happen, until it happened to me.

ACTION ADVENTURE
When I rode onto the scene, everybody noticed.

BIBLE EPIC
Cecil B. DeMille couldn't have done it any better.

LATE NIGHT NEWS
It might as well have been broadcast over the airwaves.

BORING LECTURE
The biggest challenge of the day was staying awake.

FIREWORKS DISPLAY
It was spectacular.

PROFESSIONAL WRESTLING MATCH
I feel as if Hulk Hogan's been coming after me.

Music in My Life

Put an *"X"* on the first line below—somewhere between the two extremes—to indicate how you are feeling right now. Share your answers, and then repeat this process down the list. If you feel comfortable, briefly explain your response.

IN MY PERSONAL LIFE, I'M FEELING LIKE ...
Blues in the Night _____ Feeling Groovy

IN MY FAMILY LIFE, I'M FEELING LIKE ...
Stormy Weather _____ The Sound of Music

IN MY EMOTIONAL LIFE, I'M FEELING LIKE ...
The Feeling Is Gone _____ On Eagle's Wings

IN MY WORK, SCHOOL OR CAREER, I'M FEELING LIKE ...
Take This Job and Shove It _____ The Future's So Bright I Gotta Wear Shades

IN MY SPIRITUAL LIFE, I'M FEELING LIKE ...
Sounds of Silence _____ Hallelujah Chorus

My Childhood Table

Try to recall the table where you ate most of your meals as a child, and the people who sat around that table. Use the questions below to describe these significant relationships, and how they helped to shape the person you are today.

1. What was the shape of the table?
2. Where did you sit?
3. Who else was at the table?
4. If you had to describe each person with a color, what would be the color of (for instance):
    - ❑ Your father? (e.g., dark blue, because he was conservative like IBM)
    - ❑ Your mother? (e.g., light green, because she reminded me of springtime)
5. If you had to describe the atmosphere at the table with a color, what would you choose? (e.g., bright orange, because it was warm and light)
6. Who was the person at the table who praised you and made you feel special?
7. Who provided the spiritual leadership in your home?

Home Improvement

Take inventory of your own life. Bob Munger, in his booklet *My Heart—Christ's Home*, describes the areas of a person's life as the rooms of a house. Give yourself a grade on each room as follows, then share with the others your best and worst grade.

❑ A = excellent   ❑ C = passing, needs a little dusting
❑ B = good   ❑ D = passing, but needs a lot of improvement

LIBRARY: This room is in your mind—what you allow to go into it and come out of it. It is the "control room" of the entire house.

DINING ROOM: Appetites, desires; those things your mind and spirit feed on for nourishment.

DRAWING ROOM: This is where you draw close to God—seeking time with him daily, not just in times of distress or need.

WORKSHOP: This room is where your gifts, talents and skills are put to work for God—by the power of the Spirit.

RUMPUS ROOM: The social area of your life; the things you do to amuse yourself and others.

HALL CLOSET: The one secret place that no one knows about, but is a real stumbling block in your walk in the Spirit.

How Is It With Your Soul?

John Wesley, the founder of the Methodist Church, asked his "class meetings" to check in each week at their small group meeting with this question: "How is it with your soul?" To answer this question, choose one of these four allegories to explain the past week in your life:

WEATHER: For example: "This week has been mostly cloudy, with some thunderstorms at midweek. Right now, the weather is a little brighter ..."

MUSIC: For example: "This past week has been like heavy rock music—almost too loud. The sound seems to reverberate off the walls."

COLOR: For example: "This past week has been mostly fall colors—deep orange, flaming red and pumpkin."

SEASON OF THE YEAR: For example: "This past week has been like springtime. New signs of life are beginning to appear on the barren trees, and a few shoots of winter wheat are breaking through the frozen ground."

My Spiritual Journey

The half-finished sentences below are designed to help you share your spiritual story. Ask one person to finish all the sentences. Then move to the next person, etc. If you are short on time, have only one person tell their story in this session.

1. RELIGIOUS BACKGROUND: My spiritual story begins in my home as a child, where the religious training was ...

2. CHURCH: The church that I went to as a child was ...

3. SIGNIFICANT PERSON: The person who had the greatest influence on my spiritual formation was ...

4. PERSONAL ENCOUNTER: The first time God became more than just a name to me was when ...

5. JOURNEY: Since my personal encounter with God, my Christian life might be described as ...

6. PRESENT: On a scale from 1 to 10, I would describe my spiritual energy level right now as a ...

7. NEXT STEP: The thing I need to work on right now in my spiritual life is ...

Bragging Rights

Check your group for bragging rights in these categories.

❐ SPEEDING TICKETS: the person with the most speeding tickets
❐ BROKEN BONES: the person with the most broken bones
❐ STITCHES: the person with the most stitches
❐ SCARS: the person with the longest scar
❐ FISH OR GAME: the person who claims they caught the largest fish or killed the largest animal
❐ STUNTS: the person with the most death-defying story
❐ IRON: the person who can pump the most iron

Personal Habits

Have everyone in your group finish the sentence on the first category by putting an "**X**" somewhere between the two extremes (e.g., on HOUSEWORK ... I would put myself closer to "Where's the floor?"). Repeat this process down the list as time permits.

ON HOUSEWORK, I AM SOMEWHERE BETWEEN:
Eat off the floor_____Where's the floor?

ON COOKING, I AM SOMEWHERE BETWEEN:
Every meal is an act of worship_____Make it fast and hold the frills

ON EXERCISING, I AM SOMEWHERE BETWEEN:
Workout every morning_____Click the remote

ON SHOPPING, I AM SOMEWHERE BETWEEN:
Shop all day for a bargain_____Only the best

ON EATING, I AM SOMEWHERE BETWEEN:
You are what you eat_____Eat, drink and be merry

American Graffiti

If Hollywood made a movie about your life on the night of your high school prom, what would be needed? Let each person in your group have a few minutes to recall these details. If you have more than four or five in your group, ask everyone to choose two or three topics to talk about.

1. LOCATION: Where were you living?
2. WEIGHT: How much did you weigh—soaking wet?
3. PROM: Where was it held?
4. DATE: Who did you go with?
5. CAR / TRANSPORTATION: How did you get there?
   (If you used a car, what was the model, year, color, condition?)
6. ATTIRE: What did you wear?
7. PROGRAM: What was the entertainment?
8. AFTERWARD: What did you do afterward?
9. HIGHLIGHT: What was the highlight of the evening?
10. HOMECOMING: If you could go back and visit your high school, who would you like to see?

Group Orchestra

Read out loud the first item and let everyone nominate the person in your group for this musical instrument in your group orchestra. Then, read aloud the next instrument, and call out another name, etc.

ANGELIC HARP: Soft, gentle, melodious, wooing with heavenly sounds.

OLD-FASHIONED WASHBOARD: Nonconforming, childlike and fun.

PLAYER PIANO: Mischievous, raucous, honky-tonk—delightfully carefree.

KETTLEDRUM: Strong, vibrant, commanding when needed but usually in the background.

PASSIONATE CASTANET: Full of Spanish fervor—intense and always upbeat.

STRADIVARIUS VIOLIN: Priceless, exquisite, soul-piercing—with the touch of the master.

FLUTTERING FLUTE: Tender, lighthearted, wide-ranging and clear as crystal.

SCOTTISH BAGPIPES: Forthright, distinctive and unmistakable.

SQUARE DANCE FIDDLE: Folksy, down-to-earth, toe-tapping—sprightly and full of energy.

ENCHANTING OBOE: Haunting, charming, disarming—even the cobra is harmless with this sound.

MELLOW CELLO: Deep, sonorous, compassionate—adding body and depth to the orchestra.

PIPE ORGAN: Grand, magnificent, rich—versatile and commanding.

HERALDING TRUMPET: Stirring, lively, invigorating—signaling attention and attack.

CLASSICAL GUITAR: Contemplative, profound, thoughtful *and* thought-provoking.

ONE-MAN BAND: Able to do many things well, all at once.

COMB AND TISSUE PAPER: Makeshift, original, uncomplicated—homespun and creative.

SWINGING TROMBONE: Warm, rich—great in solo or background support.

Broadway Show

Imagine for a moment that your group has been chosen to produce a Broadway show, and you have to choose people from your group for all of the jobs for this production. Have someone read out loud the job description for the first job below—PRODUCER. Then, let everyone in your group call out the name of the person in your group who would best fit this job. (You don't have to agree.) Then read the job description for the next job and let everyone nominate another person, etc. You only have 10 minutes for this assignment, so move fast.

PRODUCER: Typical Hollywood business tycoon; extravagant, big-budget, big-production magnate in the Steven Spielberg style.

DIRECTOR: Creative, imaginative brains who coordinates the production and draws the best out of others.

HEROINE: Beautiful, captivating, everybody's heart throb; defenseless when men are around, but nobody's fool.

HERO: Tough, macho, champion of the underdog, knight in shining armor; defender of truth.

COMEDIAN: Childlike, happy-go-lucky, outrageously funny, keeps everyone laughing.

CHARACTER PERSON: Rugged individualist, outrageously different, colorful, adds spice to any surrounding.

FALL GUY: Easy-going, nonchalant character who wins the hearts of everyone by being the "foil" of the heavy characters.

TECHNICAL DIRECTOR: The genius for "sound and lights"; creates the perfect atmosphere.

COMPOSER OF LYRICS: Communicates in music what everybody understands; heavy into feelings, moods, outbursts of energy.

PUBLICITY AGENT: Advertising and public relations expert; knows all the angles, good at one-liners, a flair for "hot" news.

VILLAIN: The "bad guy" who really is the heavy for the plot, forces others to think, challenges traditional values; out to destroy anything artificial or hypocritical.

AUTHOR: Shy, aloof; very much in touch with feelings, sensitive to people, puts into words what others only feel.

STAGEHAND: Supportive, behind-the-scenes person who makes things run smoothly; patient and tolerant.

Wild Predictions

Try to match the people in your group to the crazy forecasts below. (Don't take it too seriously; it's meant to be fun!) Read out loud the first item and ask everyone to call out the name of the person who is most likely to accomplish this feat. Then, read the next item and ask everyone to make a new prediction, etc.

THE PERSON IN OUR GROUP MOST LIKELY TO ...

Make a million selling Beanie Babies over the Internet

Become famous for designing new attire for sumo wrestlers

Replace Vanna White on *Wheel of Fortune*

Appear on *The Tonight Show* to exhibit an acrobatic talent

Move to a desert island

Discover a new use for underarm deodorant

Succeed David Letterman as host of *The Late Show*

Substitute for John Madden as Fox's football color analyst

Appear on the cover of *Muscle & Fitness Magazine*

Become the newest member of the Spice Girls

Work as a bodyguard for Rush Limbaugh at Feminist convention

Write a best-selling novel based on their love life

Be a dance instructor on a cruise ship for wealthy, well-endowed widows

Win the blue ribbon at the state fair for best Rocky Mountain oyster recipe

Land a job as head librarian for Amazon.com

Be the first woman to win the Indianapolis 500

Open the Clouseau Private Detective Agency

Career Placements

Read the list of career choices aloud and quickly choose someone in your group for each job—based upon their unique gifts and talents. Have fun!

SPACE ENVIRONMENTAL ENGINEER: in charge of designing the bathrooms on space shuttles

SCHOOL BUS DRIVER: for junior high kids in New York City (earplugs supplied)

WRITER: of an "advice to the lovelorn" column in Hollywood

SUPERVISOR: of a complaint department for a large automobile dealership and service department

ANIMAL PSYCHIATRIST: for French poodles in a fashionable suburb of Paris

RESEARCH SCIENTIST: studying the fertilization patterns of the dodo bird—now extinct

SAFARI GUIDE: in the heart of Africa—for wealthy widows and eccentric bachelors

LITTLE LEAGUE BASEBALL COACH: in Mudville, Illinois—last year's record was 0 and 12

MANAGER: of your local McDonald's during the holiday rush with 210 teenage employees

LIBRARIAN: for the Walt Disney Hall of Fame memorabilia

CHOREOGRAPHER: for the Dallas Cowboys cheerleaders

NURSE'S AIDE: at a home for retired Sumo wrestlers

SECURITY GUARD: crowd control officer at a rock concert

ORGANIZER: of paperwork for Congress

PUBLIC RELATIONS MANAGER: for Dennis Rodman

BODYGUARD: for Rush Limbaugh on a speaking tour of feminist groups

TOY ASSEMBLY PERSON: for a toy store over the holidays

You and Me, Partner

Think of the people in your group as you read over the list of activities below. If you had to choose someone from your group to be your partner, who would you choose to do these activities with? Jot down each person's name beside the activity. You can use each person's name only once and you have to use everyone's name once—so think it through before you jot down their names. Then, let one person listen to what others chose for them. Then, move to the next person, etc., around your group.

WHO WOULD YOU CHOOSE FOR THE FOLLOWING?

_____ ENDURANCE DANCE CONTEST partner

_____ BOBSLED RACE partner for the Olympics

_____ TRAPEZE ACT partner

_____ MY UNDERSTUDY for my debut in a Broadway musical

_____ BEST MAN or MAID OF HONOR at my wedding

_____ SECRET UNDERCOVER AGENT copartner

_____ BODYGUARD for me when I strike it rich

_____ MOUNTAIN CLIMBING partner in climbing Mt. Everest

_____ ASTRONAUT to fly the space shuttle while I walk in space

_____ SAND CASTLE TOURNAMENT building partner

_____ PIT CREW foreman for entry in Indianapolis 500

_____ AUTHOR for my biography

_____ SURGEON to operate on me for a life-threatening cancer

_____ NEW BUSINESS START-UP partner

_____ TAG-TEAM partner for a professional wrestling match

_____ HEAVY-DUTY PRAYER partner

My Gourmet Group

Here's a chance to pass out some much deserved praise for the people who have made your group something special. Ask one person to sit in silence while the others explain the delicacy they would choose to describe the contribution this person has made to your group. Repeat the process for each member of the group.

CAVIAR: That special touch of class and aristocratic taste that has made the rest of us feel like royalty.

PRIME RIB: Stable, brawny, macho, the generous mainstay of any menu; juicy, mouth-watering "perfect cut" for good nourishment.

IMPORTED CHEESE: Distinctive, tangy, mellow with age; adds depth to any meal.

VINEGAR AND OIL: Tart, witty, dry; a rare combination of healing ointment and pungent spice to add "bite" to the salad.

ARTICHOKE HEARTS: Tender and disarmingly vulnerable; whets the appetite for heartfelt sharing.

FRENCH PASTRY: Tempting, irresistible "creme de la creme" dessert; the connoisseur's delight for topping off a meal.

PHEASANT UNDER GLASS: Wild, totally unique, a rare dish for people who appreciate original fare.

CARAFE OF WINE: Sparkling, effervescent, exuberant and joyful; outrageously free and liberating to the rest of us.

ESCARGOT AND OYSTERS: Priceless treasures of the sea once out of their shells; succulent, delicate and irreplaceable.

FRESH FRUIT: Vine-ripened, energy-filled, invigorating; the perfect treat after a heavy meal.

ITALIAN ICE CREAMS: Colorful, flavorful, delightfully childlike; the unexpected surprise in our group.

Thank You

How would you describe your experience with this group? Choose one of the animals below that best describes how your experience in this group affected your life. Then share your responses with the group.

WILD EAGLE: You have helped to heal my wings, and taught me how to soar again.

TOWERING GIRAFFE: You have helped me to hold my head up and stick my neck out, and reach over the fences I have built.

PLAYFUL PORPOISE: You have helped me to find a new freedom and a whole new world to play in.

COLORFUL PEACOCK: You have told me that I'm beautiful; I've started to believe it, and it's changing my life.

SAFARI ELEPHANT: I have enjoyed this new adventure, and I'm not going to forget it, or this group; I can hardly wait for the next safari.

LOVABLE HIPPOPOTAMUS: You have let me surface and bask in the warm sunshine of God's love.

LANKY LEOPARD: You have helped me to look closely at myself and see some spots, and you still accept me the way I am.

DANCING BEAR: You have taught me to dance in the midst of pain, and you have helped me to reach out and hug again.

ALL-WEATHER DUCK: You have helped me to celebrate life—even in stormy weather—and to sing in the rain.

Academy Awards

You have had a chance to observe the gifts and talents of the members of your group. Now you will have a chance to pass out some much deserved praise for the contribution that each member of the group has made to your life. Read out loud the first award. Then let everyone nominate the person they feel is the most deserving for that award. Then read the next award, etc., through the list. Have fun!

SPARK PLUG AWARD: for the person who ignited the group

DEAR ABBY AWARD: for the person who cared enough to listen

ROYAL GIRDLE AWARD: for the person who supported us

WINNIE THE POOH AWARD: for the warm, caring person when someone needed a hug

ROCK OF GIBRALTER AWARD: for the person who was strong in the tough times of our group

OPRAH AWARD: for the person who asked the fun questions that got us to talk

TED KOPPEL AWARD: for the person who asked the heavy questions that made us think

KING ARTHUR'S AWARD: for the knight in shining armor

PINK PANTHER AWARD: for the detective who made us deal with Scripture

NOBEL PEACE PRIZE: for the person who harmonized our differences of opinion without diminishing anyone

BIG MAC AWARD: for the person who showed the biggest hunger for spiritual things

SERENDIPITY CROWN: for the person who grew the most spiritually during the course—in your estimation

You Remind Me of Jesus

Every Christian reflects the character of Jesus in some way. As your group has gotten to know each other, you can begin to see how each person demonstrates Christ in their very own personality. Go around the circle and have each person listen while others take turns telling that person what they notice in him or her that reminds them of Jesus. You may also want to tell them why you selected what you did.

YOU REMIND ME OF ...

JESUS THE HEALER: You seem to be able to touch someone's life with your compassion and help make them whole.

JESUS THE SERVANT: There's nothing that you wouldn't do for someone.

JESUS THE PREACHER: You share your faith in a way that challenges and inspires people.

JESUS THE LEADER: As Jesus had a plan for the disciples, you are able to lead others in a way that honors God.

JESUS THE REBEL: By doing the unexpected, you remind me of Jesus' way of revealing God in unique, surprising ways.

JESUS THE RECONCILER: Like Jesus, you have the ability to be a peacemaker between others.

JESUS THE TEACHER: You have a gift for bringing light and understanding to God's Word.

JESUS THE CRITIC: You have the courage to say what needs to be said, even if it isn't always popular.

JESUS THE SACRIFICE: Like Jesus, you seem willing to sacrifice anything to glorify God.

Reflections

Take some time to evaluate the life of your group by using the statements below. Read the first sentence out loud and ask everyone to explain where they would put a dot between the two extremes. When you are finished, go back and give your group an overall grade in the category of Group Building, Bible Study and Mission.

◇ GROUP BUILDING

On celebrating life and having fun together, we were more like a ...
wet blanket _____ hot tub

On becoming a caring community, we were more like a ...
prickly porcupine_____cuddly teddy bear

📖 BIBLE STUDY

On sharing our spiritual stories, we were more like a ...
shallow pond _____spring-fed lake

On digging into Scripture, we were more like a ...
slow-moving snail _____voracious anteater

◯ MISSION

On inviting new people into our group, we were more like a ...
barbed-wire fence_____wide-open door

On stretching our vision for mission, we were more like an ...
ostrich _____eagle

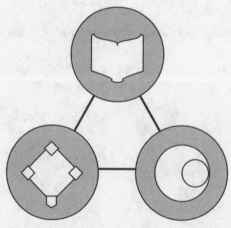

Human Bingo / Party Mixer

After the leader says "Go!" circulate the room, asking people the things described in the boxes. If someone answers "Yes" to a question, have them sign their initials in that box. Continue until someone completes the entire card—or one row if you don't have that much time. You can only use someone's name twice, and you cannot use your own name on your card.

can juggle	TP'd a house	never used an outhouse	sings in the shower	rec'd 6+ traffic tickets	paddled in school	watches Sesame Street
sleeps in church regularly	never changed a diaper	split pants in public	milked a cow	born out of the country	has been to Hawaii	can do the splits
watches soap operas	can touch tongue to nose	rode a motor-cycle	never ridden a horse	moved twice last year	sleeps on a waterbed	has hole in sock
walked in wrong restroom	loves classical music	skipped school	**FREE**	broke a leg	has a hot tub	loves eating sushi
is an only child	loves raw oysters	has a 3-inch + scar	doesn't wear PJ's	smoked a cigar	can dance the Charleston	weighs under 110 lbs.
likes writing poetry	still has tonsils	loves crossword puzzles	likes bubble baths	wearing Fruit of the Loom	doesn't use mouth-wash	often watches cartoons
kissed on first date	can wiggle ears	can play the guitar	plays chess regularly	reads the comics first	can touch palms to floor	sleeps with stuffed animal

Group Covenant

Any group can benefit from creating a group covenant. Reserve some time during one of the first meetings to discuss answers to the following questions. When everyone in the group has the same expectations for the group, everything runs more smoothly.

1. The purpose of our group is:

2. The goals of our group are:

3. We will meet for _____ weeks, after which we will decide if we wish to continue as a group. If we do decide to continue, we will reconsider this covenant.

4. We will meet _____ (weekly, every other week, monthly).

5. Our meetings will be from _____ o'clock to _____ o'clock, and we will strive to start and end on time.

6. We will meet at _____ or rotate from house to house.

7. We will take care of the following details: ❐ child care   ❐ refreshments

8. We agree to the following rules for our group:

   ❐ PRIORITY: While we are in this group, group meetings have priority.

   ❐ PARTICIPATION: Everyone is given the right to their own opinion and all questions are respected.

   ❐ CONFIDENTIALITY: Anything said in the meeting is not to be repeated outside the meeting.

   ❐ EMPTY CHAIR: The group stays open to new people and invites prospective members to visit the group.

   ❐ SUPPORT: Permission is given to call each other in times of need.

   ❐ ADVICE GIVING: Unsolicited advice is not allowed.

   ❐ MISSION: We will do all that is in our power to start a new group.

5:43 "Love your neighbor." Jesus quotes Leviticus 19:18, which was the basis for community relationships among the Israelites ("Do not seek revenge or bear a grudge against one of your people, but love your neighbor as yourself").

"hate your enemy." This command is found neither in the Old Testament nor in the Talmud. Some Old Testament passages even call for compassion toward enemies (see Prov. 25:21). However, passages that spoke of God's ultimate judicial action upon those nations which threatened Israel (see Deut. 7:1–2; 20:16–18; 23:5–6; Ps. 139:21) may have been misapplied in popular thought to justify personal animosity against those one disliked, especially non-Jews.

5:44 Love your enemies. Jesus expands Leviticus 19:18 to include all people in the call to love others. He makes it clear there is no one who stands outside the circle of love. He redefines the whole concept of who one's neighbor is (see Luke 10:25–37).

Love. The word used here is *agape.* This is love that shows itself not by what a person feels, but by what that person does. *Agape* love is benevolent action done on the behalf of another without the expectation of reward.

pray. One way this sort of love is demonstrated is by prayer for those who harass you.

5:45 Such an attitude shows one to be a child of God, because God treats all people with care, whether they are friend or enemy.

5:46 tax collectors. Tax collectors grew rich by charging people more than what was required (only *they* knew what was demanded by Rome), keeping the excess for themselves. A tax collector was, therefore, considered to be a traitor to Israel, one who was made unclean by his contact with Gentiles.

5:48 Be perfect. The Greek word used for "perfect" is *teleios,* which means "having attained the end or purpose." "A thing is perfect if it fully realizes the purpose for which it was planned, and designed, and made" (Barclay). Therefore, people can be "perfect" if they realize that for which they were made. In the creation account in the Old Testament, the purpose of men and women is stated: "God said, 'Let us make man in our image, in our likeness ... ' " (Gen. 1:26). Thus, men and women are "perfect" when they live out God's ways and so demonstrate that they are made in his image. God's way is defined here as the way of love. This commandment to be perfect defines the goal toward which God's children strive. It is not a goal they can ever reach (only God is and can be "perfect"); it is, however, a pattern that becomes the basis of how they seek to live.

Loving One's Enemies

For people living under oppression, there may be no more disheartening words in the Bible than Jesus' command to "love your enemies." At first hearing, these words sound harsh and insensitive. Oppressed people long for release from the power of their enemies, for wrongs to be made right, and (if they will admit it) for the pleasure of seeing their oppressors humiliated as they themselves have been.

But those who have tried to live out these words of Jesus know that they are true and powerful. Perhaps no one in the twentieth century has loved his enemies more courageously than Dr. Martin Luther King, Jr. The famed civil rights leader understood how difficult this kind of forgiving love was. But he also saw clearly that the alternative had wide-ranging repercussions: "Returning hate for hate multiplies hate, adding deeper darkness to a night already devoid of stars."

Hate hurts both the enemy and the victim, he said. The enemy is more than the evil deeds he does, and there is good to be found in even our worst enemy, King wrote. But hate also "scars the soul and distorts the personality" of the one who hates.[1]

When Jesus said, "I tell you: Love your enemies," his first listeners knew that he was speaking from experience. Jesus knew what it was like to be despised and rejected. Everywhere he went, he faced criticism, ridicule, and devious plots to lure him into saying or doing something that could be used against him in court. The religious leaders tried to find evidence that he had broken the Law. They "charged" him with blasphemy (Luke 5:21), failing to fast (Luke 5:33), collecting food on the Sabbath (Luke 6:2), and healing on the Sabbath (Luke 6:7,11).

Later, these same listeners would see Jesus live out these words through trial, persecution, and finally death on the cross. Yet, among his final words was a prayer for his enemies: "Father, forgive them, for they do not know what they are doing" (Luke 23:34).

[1]King, Martin Luther, Jr., *Strength to Love,* Harper and Row, 1963, pp. 34–40.

7 Giving to the Needy—Matt. 6:1–4

THREE-PART AGENDA

ICE-BREAKER
15 Minutes

BIBLE STUDY
30 Minutes

CARING TIME
15–45 Minutes

> *LEADER: If you haven't already, now is the time to begin the process of identifying an Apprentice / Leader to start a new small group (see page M6 in the center section). Check the list of ice-breakers on page M7, especially if you have a new person in this session.*

TO BEGIN THE BIBLE STUDY TIME
(Choose 1 or 2)

1. If you had $10,000 to give to a charity, what organization would you give it to and why?

2. Who in your family keeps the checkbook? Does the right hand know what the left is doing?

3. If you were involved with a play, would you rather be behind the scenes or up on stage and why?

READ SCRIPTURE & DISCUSS
(If you don't have time for all the questions in this section, conclude the Bible Study [30 min.] by answering question #8.)

The Sermon on the Mount now moves to specific areas of religious practice in which Jesus calls his disciples to an expression of righteousness that surpasses that of the Pharisees.

1. When have you been needy—a time you needed financial help?

2. How does your church handle the process of giving? How does that compare to other churches?

Giving to the Needy

6 *"Be careful not to do your 'acts of righteousness' before men, to be seen by them. If you do, you will have no reward from your Father in heaven.*

²*"So when you give to the needy, do not announce it with trumpets, as the hypocrites do in the synagogues and on the streets, to be honored by men. I tell you the truth, they have received their reward in full. ³But when you give to the needy, do not let your left hand know what your right hand is doing, ⁴so that your giving may be in secret. Then your Father, who sees what is done in secret, will reward you."*

3. How would you define "acts of righteousness"?

4. What does hypocrisy look like? (Give an example.)

5. On a scale of 1 (out of obligation) to 10 (out of joy), how would you rate your usual attitude toward giving?

6. What does this passage tell you about the approach Jesus wants us to have toward giving (see note on verse 3)?

7. In what ways have you given of your time and talent to the work of God's kingdom? Is there a new area of ministry that you would like to try?

8. Think of someone who is needy, spiritually or physically. What can you or this group do to help that person in the coming week?

CARING TIME
(Choose 1 or 2 of these questions before taking prayer requests and closing in prayer. Be sure to pray for the empty chair.)

1. You are over halfway through this study and it's time for a check-up—how are you feeling?

2. What is something for which you are particularly thankful?

3. How can the group pray for you this week?

Notes—Matthew 6:1–4

Summary. Throughout 5:21–48, Jesus contrasted the righteousness of the scribes and Pharisees with that of his followers in terms of their attitudes toward general ethical practices. In 6:1–18, he shows how the surpassing righteousness (5:20) he is calling for relates to three specific examples of common Jewish piety: almsgiving (6:1–4), prayer (6:5–15), and fasting (6:16–18). In each case, Jesus first identifies the wrong way to go about such acts of devotion, and then he gives the right way.

6:1 Jesus first defines in general terms what one must not do—namely, not make a public display of religious devotion.

"acts of righteousness." This is the same word found in 5:20, but the context indicates that the emphasis is on the religious activities commonly associated with moral righteousness. While there were a variety of Jewish sects which emphasized different points of faith and practice, all sects observed the three marks of righteousness spoken of in 6:1–18. The fact that Jesus' disciples did *not* practice fasting (like the Pharisees or the disciples of John the Baptist) was a point of criticism by those who could not conceive of a religious devotion that was not marked by this practice (Mark 2:18ff).

to be seen by them. "At first sight these words appear to contradict (Jesus') earlier command to 'let your light shine before men, that they may see … ' (5:16). In both verses he speaks of doing good works 'before men' and in both the objective is stated, namely in order to be 'seen' by them. But in the earlier case he commands it, while in the latter one he prohibits it. How can this discrepancy be resolved? … The clue lies in the fact that Jesus is speaking against different sins. It is our human cowardice which made him say 'let your light shine before men,' and our human vanity which made him tell us to beware of practicing our piety before men. A.B. Bruce sums it up well when he writes that we are to '*show* when tempted to hide' and '*hide* when tempted to show.' Our good works must be public so that our light shines; our religious devotions must be secret lest we boast about them" (Stott).

reward. The reward from the Father is the fullness of the kingdom (5:3). This is not something one *earns* by performing secret acts of righteousness; rather, it is a gift *given* to those who recognize their

spiritual poverty. Those who perform acts of religious devotion in order to impress God and others show that they have not yet come to grips with their spiritual bankruptcy. Thus, there is no promise from God for them. In contrast, true almsgiving, prayer and fasting is a mark of one's grateful, heartfelt response to God's graciousness and mercy. To such people the promise of the kingdom is given.

6:2–4 One of the most important first-century religious duties was giving to the poor. Jesus uses a couple of humorous images to communicate that this must not be done with the desire to be congratulated by others or even oneself. It should not be a self-centered matter, but rather an act that simply reflects one's inner loyalty to God.

6:2 ***announce it with trumpets.*** At certain feast times, trumpets would be blown as a way of calling people to gather for the feast. At other occasions, such as in times of famine, a trumpet would be blown so that the poor might know where to gather in order to receive food donated by a wealthy person. However, the blowing of horns before giving alms was not a regular event. Jesus uses the image metaphorically (like our phrase "he's just blowing his own horn") to accent the ostentatious display certain people made when they made their contributions. Their concern was not with glorifying God nor with caring for the needy, but with making sure that others knew they were performing their religious obligations.

the hypocrites. This is a favorite term for Matthew, who uses it 13 times (e.g., 7:5; 15:7–9; 22:18; 23:13–29). While most translations and commentaries translate this like the NIV version, Albright and Mann make a strong case that the term in Jesus' day did not connote the idea of a play-actor which we typically think of as a hypocrite. In Jesus' day, they contend, the word carried the sense of one who was overly scrupulous. In 7:5 and 15:7–9, for example, the Pharisees' preoccupation with the details of their tradition blinded them to the fact that they were in reality violating God's Law. The point is that the Pharisees were not being rebuked for consciously playing a role they knew did not match their real beliefs, but for failing to see the forest (the intent of God's Law) because of their preoccupation with the trees (the details of their traditions). In this incident, it was not their lack of inner conviction that

Jesus is faulting (they undoubtedly sincerely believed they ought to give to the poor), but the fact they wanted to make sure that their scrupulous observance of the traditions was seen by others.

they have received their reward in full. A sense of smug self-satisfaction and temporary honor received from others they have impressed is the only reward these people will get. There is nothing eternal or spiritual about it whatsoever.

6:3 *do not let your left hand know what your right hand is doing.* This is another humorous, graphic illustration used to stress the point that giving is to be viewed as an act between the giver and God. The issue is not whether one gives in public versus in private, but the attitude with which one gives at all. The point of this teaching is not to rule out the pledge systems frequently used by churches so that they can form responsible budgets, nor to invalidate the importance of discussion in a family about its giving priorities. What is rejected here is the motivation of giving with the calculated desire to prove to others (v. 2) *or* to oneself (vv. 3–4) that one is righteous. While the gift still is of use to the recipient, under those types of circumstances it has no value for the person who gave. In contrast, the proper attitude for giving is seen in the story of the poor widow who, with no thought of impressing others nor any pretensions about being able to earn anything from God, gave all she could for the sake of others out of a heart of love and gratitude (Luke 21:1–4).

6:4 *in secret.* This reinforces the unselfconscious giving reflected in verse 3 about not letting the left hand know what the right hand is doing. "What is it to perform acts of love in secret? The secret place is the centered place … to be contrasted with the merely external dimension of human existence. From beginning to end, the Sermon on the Mount attempts to draw the distinction between the center and the periphery of human existence: the central problem to be confronted is not murder, but the anger of the soul; the crucial problem is not adultery and divorce, but the attitude of the lustful heart; and since this is so, when acts of charity are performed,

the most important fact about them is not their external expression, but the centered self from which they spring. Where do acts of charity originate? Jesus tells us that if they are to be authentic, they must originate from the secret place … the centered place where God himself promises to be present" (Vaught).

On Rewards …

Nobody talks very much about heavenly rewards these days, at least not in Western countries. Pride keeps some people from admitting they need or desire anything more than they already have. A false understanding of humility makes others believe it's wrong even to think about being rewarded by God.

Perhaps the problem lies in a confusion about the difference between *rewards* and *earnings*. Of course, no one can *earn* God's acceptance by good works. Salvation is a "gift of God"; it is "not by works" (Eph. 2:8–9). The Christian's good works are to be an expression of thanks to God for what God has already done in Christ, not payment for a ticket into his presence. God also freely expresses his appreciation through gifts of love. Throughout Scripture, God promises that he will reward, or "bless," those who are faithful.

C.S. Lewis, in reflecting on Jesus' promise of rewards in Matthew 6:1–4, puts the matter of rewards into a proper perspective:

> *"If we consider the unblushing promises of reward and the staggering nature of rewards promised in the Gospels, it would seem that our Lord finds our desires, not too strong, but too weak. We are half-hearted creatures, fooling about with drink and sex and ambition when infinite joy is offered us, like an ignorant child who wants to go on making mud pies in a slum because he cannot imagine what is meant by the offer of a holiday at the sea. We are far too easily pleased"* (C.S. Lewis, *The Weight of Glory*, Eerdmans, 1975).

8 Prayer / Fasting—Matthew 6:5–18

THREE-PART AGENDA

ICE-BREAKER
15 Minutes

BIBLE STUDY
30 Minutes

CARING TIME
15–45 Minutes

LEADER: *Have you started working with your group about your mission—for instance, by having them review page M3 in the center section? If you have a new person at the meeting, remember to do an appropriate ice-breaker from the center section.*

TO BEGIN THE BIBLE STUDY TIME
(Choose 1 or 2)

1. What prayers do you remember from your childhood?

2. What is the longest you have gone without eating?

3. When it comes to praying out loud in front of people, how comfortable are you?

READ SCRIPTURE & DISCUSS
(If you don't have time for all the questions in this section, conclude the Bible Study [30 min.] by answering question #8.)

1. When do you pray: Before meals? Before bed? In a crisis? In daily devotions? At small group? Other?

2. Where do you go when you need to pray? What do you find yourself praying for most often?

3. Using the prayer (known as the Lord's Prayer) as a model, what three things related to God are expressed first (vv. 9–10)? What three things related to our needs are expressed next (vv. 11–13)?

4. What do verses 12,14 and 15 say to you about the relationship between forgiving and being forgiven?

Prayer

[5]*"And when you pray, do not be like the hypocrites, for they love to pray standing in the synagogues and on the street corners to be seen by men. I tell you the truth, they have received their reward in full.* [6]*But when you pray, go into your room, close the door and pray to your Father, who is unseen. Then your Father, who sees what is done in secret, will reward you.* [7]*And when you pray, do not keep on babbling like pagans, for they think they will be heard because of their many words.* [8]*Do not be like them, for your Father knows what you need before you ask him.*

[9]*"This, then, is how you should pray:*

> *" 'Our Father in heaven,*
> *hallowed be your name,*
> [10]*your kingdom come,*
> *your will be done*
> *on earth as it is in heaven.*
> [11]*Give us today our daily bread.*
> [12]*Forgive us our debts,*
> *as we also have forgiven our debtors.*
> [13]*And lead us not into temptation,*
> *but deliver us from the evil one.*[a]*'*

[14]*For if you forgive men when they sin against you, your heavenly Father will also forgive you.* [15]*But if you do not forgive men their sins, your Father will not forgive your sins.*

Fasting

[16]*"When you fast, do not look somber as the hypocrites do, for they disfigure their faces to show men they are fasting. I tell you the truth, they have received their reward in full.* [17]*But when you fast, put oil on your head and wash your face,* [18]*so that it will not be obvious to men that you are fasting, but only to your Father, who is unseen; and your Father, who sees what is done in secret, will reward you."*

[a]13 Or *from evil*; some late manuscripts *one, / for yours is the kingdom and the power and the glory forever. Amen.*

5. What is the purpose of fasting? In what situations you face might fasting be helpful?

6. On a scale of 1 (never) to 10 (regularly), rank yourself on the practice of the spiritual discipline of prayer and of fasting.

7. In praying, what do you find is your biggest challenge?

8. In getting serious about your spiritual life, what is something you need to start doing?

CARING TIME
(Choose 1 or 2 of these questions before taking prayer requests and closing in prayer. Be sure to pray for the empty chair.)

1. Have you started working on your group mission—to choose an Apprentice / Leader from your group to start a new group in the future? (See Mission / Multiplication on page M3.)

2. As a group, recite the Lord's Prayer together.

3. How can the group pray for you this week?

6:5–15 Jesus now focuses attention on prayer, a second common element found in all forms of Jewish piety (see "Summary" note and note on 6:1, p. 36).

6:5 *the hypocrites.* See note on 6:2 (p. 36).

synagogues / street corners. Pious Jews would recite certain prayers at sunrise, at 9 a.m., at noon, at 3 p.m. (Acts 3:1), and at sunset. When the appointed hour for prayer came, they would simply stop where they were and pray. Jesus did not object to this practice in and of itself. What he was condemning was the fact that some people would make a *point* of being in a public place when it came time to pray, so that others might observe how devout they were.

they have received their reward in full. See note on 6:2 (p. 37).

6:6 *go into your room, close the door.* Jesus' point is not to do away with public prayer (which he practiced himself), but to stress that prayer is to be rooted in a desire to commune with God, not in a desire to make a public display of religiosity. Corporate, public prayer (as demonstrated throughout the history of Jewish and Christian practice) is perfectly legitimate when approached with this attitude.

in secret. See note on 6:4 (p. 37). "… the secret place was not the room, but the center of the person … seeking communion with God" (Vaught).

6:7 *do not keep on babbling like pagans.* While the conspicuous prayer habits of the Pharisees are to be rejected, so are the meaningless, repetitive prayers of the pagans. God does not need to be awakened, impressed, or persuaded by us to act in accord with our needs. Christian prayer is not an attempt to manipulate God to do our bidding. It is not the mindless and mechanical repetition of many words in an attempt to impress or assuage a deity. Instead, it is a form of communication between a person and a loving, gracious God who is already predisposed to do good to those who call upon him.

6:8 *your Father.* This is a common New Testament way of addressing and picturing God. For members of the kingdom, God is not primarily Judge (with its implication of moral censure), nor even Creator (with its sense of transcendent, impersonal power), but Father—a term meant to convey the warmth, intimacy and care that is reflected in families where the father fulfills his role as a parent. Especially in the context of the Sermon on the Mount, the image of Father is meant to convey a picture of one who lovingly provides for all our needs (5:45; 6:26,33; 7:11).

knows … before you ask. This is not meant to indicate that prayer is unimportant, but rather to stress the intimate concern and awareness God has for his people. Prayer, like a child's communication with his or her father, serves to nurture the relationship between ourselves and God as it allows us to glimpse God's heart and mind.

6:9–15 The fact that the so-called Lord's Prayer is found in a shorter form and in another context in Luke 11:2–4 indicates that it was meant more as a guide to shape our private and corporate prayers rather than as a liturgical form to be mechanically repeated in worship services. It consists of three petitions that relate to God and his kingdom and three requests that deal with the everyday needs of life as disciples pursue the kingdom. The prayer suggests the kinds of things that ought to occupy the content of the prayers of God's people.

6:9 *Our Father.* The address stresses not only intimacy with God, but also the corporate nature of the disciples' relationship with one another.

in heaven. This does not "locate" God somewhere beyond space, but stresses his majesty and dignity.

hallowed be your name. The first petition is that the name of God might be held in honor by all. The "name" of someone is a shorthand way of expressing that person's character and nature. The utmost concern for the disciple is that all he or she does is to be done to the glory of God, whose "name" he or she bears. This petition also reaches out from beyond that personal concern to include the desire that God be honored and worshiped by all peoples everywhere.

6:10 *your kingdom come.* The second petition expresses the vision that is to motivate the people of God. Their hope is rooted in the eschatological hope that God's kingdom will indeed one day be fully manifest and all people will know him to be King. To pray this petition is a revolutionary action. It expresses one's ultimate loyalty to God above all other forces that compete for the allegiance of a disciple.

your will be done. God's kingdom is in evidence wherever his will is being followed.

on earth as it is in heaven. This qualifies each of the three requests: in heaven his name is honored, his kingdom has come, and his will is done. The essence of these three requests is the heartfelt desire for this same reality to prevail here on earth.

6:11–13 The three requests reflect the disciples' dependency upon God to provide the physical, spiritual and moral resources necessary to honor God's name, pursue his kingdom, and live in accordance with his will.

6:11 *our daily bread.* The first request is for "everything necessary for the preservation of this life, like food, a healthy body, good weather, house, home … good government and peace" (Martin Luther). It reflects a day-by-day dependence upon God as the one who provides for our needs.

6:12 *Forgive us.* The second request is an acknowledgment that all people sin and thus are in need of God's daily forgiveness.

debts. Sin is seen as a debt (in that it represents a loss before God that we cannot repay).

as we also have forgiven. This is not in any way a "bargain" with God, as if the disciple is to wring forgiveness out of God by especially good behavior. It simply is a reflection that the recognition of our great debt before God is what moves us to freely forgive those who have sinned against us.

6:13 *lead us not into temptation.* The word *temptation* is better understood here as *test* or *trial.* Testings of our faith are sure to come. The request is not a plea to be exempt from the common moral struggles of life, but that God would empower the disciple to have the moral strength to resist giving in to evil during such struggles.

deliver us from the evil one. The evil one (the devil) is the real source of temptations.

6:14–15 See notes on 6:12.

6:16–18 The third and final section concerning religious obligations has to do with fasting. The issue is not whether disciples should fast. The question is how one goes about fasting. Since the purpose of fasting is to focus one's attention and energy on God, Jesus teaches that his disciples should not fast in a way so as to draw attention to themselves.

6:16 *fast.* Fasting was an important part of Jewish religious celebration. Jews fasted on the Day of Atonement as well as at other special times (see Deut. 9:9; 1 Sam. 31:13; Ps. 35:13). The Pharisees made a practice of fasting twice a week. To fast meant to abstain from food from sunup to sundown.

disfigure. Literally, this means "to make invisible." This refers to the custom when fasting of putting ashes on the head (which would dirty and cover up one's face) or covering one's face with a cloth.

their reward in full. Once again, as with giving and with prayer (6:1–2,5), those who play to the crowds and are applauded by them for being "righteous" have received all the reward they will get.

6:17 *put oil on your head and wash your face.* Oil was a commonly used cosmetic. The followers of Jesus are to give no outward indication that they are engaged in a fast.

Differences in Prayer …

"… the fundamental difference between various kinds of prayer is in the fundamentally different images of God which lie behind them. The tragic mistake of the Pharisees and pagans, of hypocrites and heathen, is to be found in their false image of God. Indeed, neither is really thinking of God at all, for the hypocrite thinks only of himself while the heathen thinks of other things. … Is God a commodity that we can use him to boost our own status, or a computer that we can feed words to him mechanically?

"… We need to remember that (God) loves his children with most tender affection, that he sees his children even in the secret place, that he knows his children and all their needs before they ask him, and that he acts on behalf of his children by his heavenly and kingly power" (John R.W. Stott, *The Message of the Sermon on the Mount,* InterVarsity, 1978, p. 152).

THREE-PART AGENDA

ICE-BREAKER
15 Minutes

BIBLE STUDY
30 Minutes

CARING TIME
15–45 Minutes

 LEADER: To help you identify an Apprentice / Leader for a new small group (or if you have a new person at this meeting), see the listing of ice-breakers on page M7 of the center section.

TO BEGIN THE BIBLE STUDY TIME
(Choose 1 or 2)

1. What types of "treasure" did you collect as a kid? What do you like to collect now?

2. What is the most valuable thing in your wallet or purse right now? How would you feel if you lost it?

3. Would you say you are more of a saver or spender?

READ SCRIPTURE & DISCUSS
(If you don't have time for all the questions in this section, conclude the Bible Study [30 min.] by answering question #8.)

Jesus now focuses on how true righteousness differs from selfish materialism.

1. What is something you own that was once shiny and new but is now old and faded?

2. In our society, how is success generally measured? From what sources do you feel pressured to meet this standard?

3. What is the difference between treasures on earth and treasures in heaven?

Treasures in Heaven

[19] *"Do not store up for yourselves treasures on earth, where moth and rust destroy, and where thieves break in and steal. [20] But store up for yourselves treasures in heaven, where moth and rust do not destroy, and where thieves do not break in and steal. [21] For where your treasure is, there your heart will be also.*

[22] *"The eye is the lamp of the body. If your eyes are good, your whole body will be full of light. [23] But if your eyes are bad, your whole body will be full of darkness. If then the light within you is darkness, how great is that darkness!*

[24] *"No one can serve two masters. Either he will hate the one and love the other, or he will be devoted to the one and despise the other. You cannot serve both God and Money."*

4. If Jesus were to analyze your life, what would he say your "treasure" is?

5. What is the connection between eye and body? What does it mean to have good eyes? Bad eyes?

6. What is Jesus saying in this passage regarding money and how we should relate to it?

7. This past week, did you feel more devoted to God or "Money"?

8. What investment can you make with your life that will pay heavenly dividends?

CARING TIME

(Choose 1 or 2 of these questions before taking prayer requests and closing in prayer. Be sure to pray for the empty chair.)

1. What is your dream for the future mission of this group?

2. Rate this past week on a scale of 1 (terrible) to 10 (great). What's the outlook for this week?

3. How can the group pray for you this week?

Notes—Matthew 6:19–24

Summary. While 6:1–18 concentrated on how true righteousness (5:20) differs from the self-serving legalism of the Pharisees, here the emphasis is on how this righteousness differs from the self-absorbed materialism of the Gentiles (6:32). Just as the knowledge that "your Father, who sees what is done in secret" (6:18) frees us from having to make a public spectacle of religious practices, so, too, the knowledge that "your heavenly Father knows that you need them" (6:32) frees us from having to be absorbed with how to provide for our material needs. Discipleship to Jesus means the believer must choose between two treasures (vv. 19–21), two visions (vv. 22–23), two masters (v. 24), and two attitudes (6:25–34).

6:19–21 In 6:1–18, the contrast is between earthly and heavenly reward. Here the contrast is between earthly and heavenly treasure.

6:19 *for yourselves.* Possessions as such are not forbidden, nor is the provision for family needs proscribed or condemned (see Prov. 6:6ff). What is incompatible with seeking God's kingdom is the obsessive pursuit of accumulating wealth or possessions as a means of trying to obtain security in life.

treasures on earth. These are any material treasures which, by their very nature, are subject to theft, corrosion, decay and loss.

moth and rust. Literally, this is "moths and eating" (Mounce). Since rich, elaborate clothes were one mark of a person's wealth, the phrase is probably meant to point out how such garments can be destroyed by moths, mice or other vermin. In the days before mothballs, cedar closets and steel safes, the irony of building one's life around one's possessions was that even the most valuable treasures on earth were vulnerable to destruction by insignificant creatures like moths and mice. Even with today's protective devices, inflation, devaluation, stock market crashes, economic shocks, etc. can despoil a person's earthly treasures literally overnight. Such treasures, by their very nature, are not permanent.

thieves. There were no security systems to prevent thieves from breaking in and stealing whatever valuables a person might try to hide in his or her house.

6:20 *treasures in heaven.* Such treasures include

"... the development of a Christlike character (since all we can take with us to heaven is ourselves); the increase of faith, hope, and charity, all of which (Paul said) 'abide' (1 Cor. 13:13); growth in the knowledge of Christ whom one day we shall see face to face; the active endeavor (by prayer and witness) to introduce others to Christ, so that they, too, may inherit eternal life; and the use of our money for Christian causes, which is the only investment whose dividends are everlasting" (Stott). Disciples "store up" these treasures by an obedient way of life.

6:21 The real issue is not about the size and amount of one's possessions, but one's devotion to them. While a wealthy person's obsession with material goods might be more obvious, people of modest means can also have their lives revolve around trying to maintain or augment the few possessions they have. "Our treasure may ... be small and inconspicuous, but its size is immaterial; it all depends on the heart. ... And if we ask how we are to know where our hearts are, the answer is ... simple—everything which hinders us from loving God above all things and acts as a barrier between ourselves and our obedience to Jesus is our treasure, and the place where our heart is" (Bonhoeffer). What people occupy themselves with reveals the intent and character of their motivations. This passage reveals that material possessions have the power to command a loyalty which rightly belongs to God.

6:22–23 The next comparison is between a good eye (literally, an eye that is "single") and a bad eye (literally, an "evil" eye).

The eye is the lamp of the body. As a light shows us the way through the darkness, so the eye is what allows us to see so that we might move and act freely. Both eye and heart are sometimes used in the Bible as a metaphor to describe the motivating principle that guides the way a person lives (e.g., note the parallelism in Psalm 119:36–37: "Turn my *heart* toward your statutes and not toward selfish gain. Turn my *eyes* away from worthless things ..."). To have a good eye is to have a pure heart. The image of an "evil eye" was used to describe those who were greedy or stingy. Thus, the "good eye" refers to people who have a generous spirit that leads them to share their material possessions. The contrast, therefore, is between those who seek the true goal which is obedience to God and those who lead "a life in the dark, like a blind man, because the 'evil eye' of selfishness gives no light to show the way" (France).

6:24 The contrast here is between competing masters. In one of his most memorable phrases, Jesus points out that it is impossible for a person to serve two masters.

serve. Literally, this is "to be a slave of." While a person might work for two employers, he or she cannot belong to two owners.

hate. This is not so much active dislike as it is a way of expressing the fact that loyalty to the one master makes loyalty to another master literally impossible.

Money. From *mamonas*, an Aramaic word that means possessions. God, who calls his people to "have no other gods before me" (Ex. 20:3), will not tolerate divided loyalty from his people. Such divided loyalty is tantamount to idolatry (Eph. 5:5).

Material World

James Paternoster says materialism is "more than just our tendency to buy more than we should. It's our tendency to buy a false world view which places material things at the center of life." He goes on to say:

"… advertising (is) one of the most powerful channels through which the seeds of materialism are sown in our lives. Advertisers work on the assumption that in a world of competing products, they must present their product as the answer to our desires, felt needs and fears.

"Admittedly some of the ads we see are fairly straightforward. Paper towels do absorb spills, and fabric softeners soften fabrics. But what about the connection between toothpaste and romance, or credit cards and the good life, or beer and meaningful friendships?

"The contrast is clear. Both paths require devotion and effort. Both are exclusive of the other. Jesus says that our needs for warmth, love, self-esteem, purpose, hope, happiness, and meaningful productivity all are met only as we seek after God and his ways above all else. Much of society is devoted to saying that such needs can be met through what we own, how much we own, and who knows what we own! As someone said, 'My whole life is spent spending money I don't have to buy things I don't want to impress people I don't like!' "

How can we combat such pervasive materialism? Paternoster offers three suggestions:

1. Expose the false pretenses in ads. "There is nothing you can buy that will give you love, bring you happiness, ensure your success or make you the person you desire to be."

2. Consciously oppose the materialistic lie by filling our minds with God's truth. "Here's a simple way to explore the conflict. Make a list of all the values and desires that you have noticed ads promoting. Now … read Matthew 5–7 and Galatians 5. List those qualities described as good and those described as evil in those passages. Then compare your two lists, noting which values and desires fall into the following categories: those commended by Jesus or Paul and featured in ads; those commended by Jesus or Paul but absent from ads; those values commended in ads but absent from or condemned by Jesus or Paul."

3. "Remember: renewing our minds is hard work. Companies with things to sell us work very hard to influence our thinking. We must work just as hard at studying God's word and spending time in conversation with him. We can help one another combat materialism by praying for each other, examining the messages we're receiving together and keeping one another accountable for our attitudes and day-to-day decisions about money … our goal is not to shun all material objects, but to enjoy them for what they truly are."[1]

Ron Sider writes of how John Wesley practiced the commitment called for in this passage. Wesley taught:

"Christians should give away all but 'the plain necessaries of life'—that is, plain, wholesome food, clean clothes and enough to carry on one's business. One should earn what one can, justly and honestly. Capital need not be given away. But all income should be given to the poor after one satisfies bare necessities.

"Wesley lived what he preached. Sales of his books often earned him 1,400 pounds annually, but he spent only 30 pounds on himself. The rest he gave away. … 'If I leave behind me 10 pounds,' he once wrote, 'you and all mankind bear witness against me that I lived and died a thief and a robber.'"[2]

[1]James Paternoster, "Materialism: Breaking Free From Madison Avenue's Grip," *Student Leadership Journal,* IVCF, Fall, 1990.
[2]Adapted from Ron Sider, *Rich Christians in an Age of Hunger,* 1990, Word, Inc.

10 Do Not Worry—Matthew 6:25–34

THREE-PART AGENDA

ICE-BREAKER
15 Minutes

BIBLE STUDY
30 Minutes

CARING TIME
15–45 Minutes

 LEADER: To help you identify an Apprentice / Leader for a new small group (or if you have a new person at this meeting), see the listing of ice-breakers on page M7 of the center section.

TO BEGIN THE BIBLE STUDY TIME
(Choose 1 or 2)

1. What is your favorite restaurant?

2. How long does it take you to get ready in the morning?

3. How often do you go shopping for clothes? Is shopping a chore or a pleasure?

READ SCRIPTURE & DISCUSS
(If you don't have time for all the questions in this section, conclude the Bible Study [30 min.] by answering question #7.)

Jesus now instructs his followers about the proper attitude towards their material needs.

1. Where do you fall on the worry scale: 1 (What, me worry?) to 10 (world-class worry wart)?

2. What is something you are prone to worry about: Finances? Kids? Work? Parents? Your spouse? The weather? Other?

3. From this passage what lesson can you learn from "bird-watching"? From stopping and smelling the flowers?

Do Not Worry

25"Therefore I tell you, do not worry about your life, what you will eat or drink; or about your body, what you will wear. Is not life more important than food, and the body more important than clothes? 26Look at the birds of the air; they do not sow or reap or store away in barns, and yet your heavenly Father feeds them. Are you not much more valuable than they? 27Who of you by worrying can add a single hour to his life^a?

28"And why do you worry about clothes? See how the lilies of the field grow. They do not labor or spin. 29Yet I tell you that not even Solomon in all his splendor was dressed like one of these. 30If that is how God clothes the grass of the field, which is here today and tomorrow is thrown into the fire, will he not much more clothe you, O you of little faith? 31So do not worry, saying, 'What shall we eat?' or 'What shall we drink?' or 'What shall we wear?' 32For the pagans run after all these things, and your heavenly Father knows that you need them. 33But seek first his kingdom and his righteousness, and all these things will be given to you as well. 34Therefore do not worry about tomorrow, for tomorrow will worry about itself. Each day has enough trouble of its own."

^a27 Or *single cubit to his height*

4. According to Jesus, what are we to seek in place of food and clothes? What results from seeking this (see v. 33)?

5. How are you at taking one day at a time? Is reading, "Each day has enough trouble of its own" (v. 34) encouraging or discouraging to you?

6. What is one thing you can do in the coming week to "seek first his kingdom and his righteousness"?

7. What worry do you need to place in God's hands and trust him with?

CARING TIME

(Choose 1 or 2 of these questions before taking prayer requests and closing in prayer. Be sure to pray for the empty chair.)

1. Who would you choose as the leader if your group "gave birth" to a new small group? Who else would you choose to be part of the leadership core for a new group?

2. Is there something for which you would like this group to help hold you accountable?

3. How can the group pray for you this week?

Summary. The implication of serving God and not Money (6:24) is that the disciple need not worry about the necessities of life (specifically, food, drink and clothing). By way of illustrating the fact that God takes care of those who follow him, Jesus notes that birds depend upon God for their food, and flowers depend on him for their beautiful adornment. His point is that God's children, who are more valuable than the birds and the flowers, can therefore depend upon God to show the same care for them that he gives to birds and plants. To worry is to show a lack of dependence on God.

6:25 *Therefore I tell you.* This passage spells out the significance of the principles Jesus laid down in 6:19–24. Since disciples of Jesus have a heavenly treasure (6:20), their eye is focused on the good things of God (6:22), and their loyalty is to God and not Money; *therefore,* they need not be anxious about the material needs of life.

do not worry. Worry or anxiety is a state of mind. Having chosen God's way, the disciple must not be overly concerned about the demands and pressures that occupy those committed to the other way (materialism).

Is not life more important than food …? The materialistic quest reduces life to a matter of keeping the body fed and dressed. While that is a necessary part of life, the materialistic answer makes this the central focus.

6:26 In showing the folly of making concern for food the central focus of life, Jesus points out how God provides for the needs of the birds. The point is not that his disciples need not do anything to feed themselves, but that their ultimate trust rests in God to meet their needs. "What is prohibited is worry, not work" (France).

much more valuable. The point of the creation story (Gen. 1) is to stress God as Creator of all and the role of humanity as God's representative on earth, charged with the responsibility to "rule" the earth (such that it is nurtured and prosperous). It is because humanity has a special relationship and responsibility to the Creator that people are "more valuable" than animals. Since God meets the needs of the animals, will he not do so for people? This does not mean that Christians are somehow exempt from the possibility of hunger or famine. The

common sufferings of humanity affect believers, too. The point of the passage is that we are fed, not by our own efforts, but by God's mercy. Hoarding and preoccupation with material concerns reflect a lack of trust in God as the ultimate provider. This is especially the case when one person (or nation) hoards goods at the expense of others. In general, it is not the earth's inability to feed its population that leads to famines, rather it is the human predilection to use food as a political weapon (or as a means of social control) that so often accounts for the mass suffering involved in famines. Those who could help hoard instead of share. The same Jesus who here promises that God feeds the hungry likewise commands his followers to be the agents through which the food is given (Matt. 25:31–46).

6:27 *a single hour.* Jesus' point is that since all the worry in the world cannot even add an hour to one's life, what is the purpose of worrying? (Modern medicine might add that worry actually will probably *reduce* one's life span through stress-related diseases!) While the older versions of the Bible rendered this "a single cubit," this translation makes more sense in this context. Even if worry *could* add a single hour to one's entire life, that would not be a very significant payoff for all the anxiety. However, if worry could actually add a cubit (about 18 inches) to one's height, that would be a major accomplishment!

6:28–30 Following through on his comment in verse 25, Jesus now encourages his followers to consider how even flowers, unable to rush about in anxious pursuit of their physical needs, are adorned with beauty. Since God provides them with such beauty, why should his people fear that they will be neglected by God?

6:29 *Solomon.* Solomon, the third king of Israel, was noted for his fabulous wealth (1 Kings 10:14–29). The folly of being anxious about clothes is revealed in that even the simplest flower is adorned more delicately and attractively than the richest man or woman.

6:30 *thrown into the fire.* Some of the flowers Jesus has in mind are not the ornamental ones most often noticed for their beauty. Even weeds that were commonly used for fuel have a beauty that far surpasses their intended use. Therefore, people can have the assurance God will not forget to provide them with needed clothes.

you of little faith. This is a single Greek word meaning "little-faiths." Matthew uses it four of the five times it appears in the New Testament (8:26; 14:31; 16:8; 17:20). As the two illustrations here show, faith is reliance on the love, care and power of God. Faith is the opposite of anxiety.

6:31 *So do not worry.* Again, what is commended here is not idleness but faith. As verse 33 indicates, the disciples of Jesus are to be busy, but their activity is centered around pursuing God's agenda; they are not to be centered around simply meeting their own needs. They are to be confident that God will meet their needs.

"What shall we eat / drink / wear?" This is the "world's Trinity of cares" (Stott).

6:33 Having described where their attention is *not* to be directed (toward worry), Jesus now tells his disciples where their focus *is* meant to be: They are to be oriented toward God's unfolding work ("his kingdom") and on acts that reflect his nature ("his righteousness"). All of one's life—from one's inner attitudes to one's social involvements—is to be brought under this overriding purpose. The supreme ambition of the Christian is that all that he or she thinks, says, and does be for the glory of God. The implication of this verse is that if a disciple is focused on finding and doing the will of God, then that disciple will not worry about material things. His or her needs are in the hands of God.

6:34 *tomorrow.* Worry generally has to do with the future, about what lies ahead. The disciple is to live one day at a time, and not in dread of what might happen in the future.

trouble. Disciples are not promised a trouble-free life; they are, however, promised God's care.

The Simple Life

Richard Foster defines this commitment to following Jesus as the discipline of *simplicity,* of living for one thing (the kingdom of God) as opposed to the fragmented loyalties of the rest of the world. He writes, "Freedom from anxiety is characterized by three inner attitudes.

- To receive what we have as a gift from God is the first inner attitude of simplicity.
- To know that it is God's business, and not ours, to care for what we have is the second inner attitude of simplicity.
- To have our goods available to others marks the third inner attitude of simplicity."

Foster goes on to say that simplicity is not only an inner attitude, it also has an outward expression. The questions below reflect seven of the overall principles Foster suggests we consider as a way of reflecting about how the way we live shows what is really central to us. These are not the only questions that could be asked, but they are helpful ones in applying the idea of simplicity to modern life.

- Do I buy things for their usefulness rather than for their status? Do I sometimes act as though my happiness is really tied up with owning some certain product ? Do I attempt to stay within my means and avoid financing schemes?
- Am I willing to reject anything that might be producing an addiction in me (i.e., a sense that I could just not do without _____)?
- Am I able to enjoy things without having to possess them as my own? In what ways am I learning the freedom of giving things away?
- Am I appreciative of the beauty of the creation?

- Are honesty and integrity the distinguishing characteristics of my speech?
- Am I free to reject anything (e.g., possessions or positions) that breeds the oppression of others?
- Do I shun whatever would distract me from my number-one priority—to seek first God's kingdom and righteousness? Do I actively cultivate attitudes and actions that would help me in this pursuit?

(Taken from *Celebration of Discipline,* Richard J. Foster, Harper & Row, 1978, pp. 77–83).

THREE-PART AGENDA

ICE-BREAKER
15 Minutes

BIBLE STUDY
30 Minutes

CARING TIME
15–45 Minutes

> *LEADER: To help you identify people who might form the core of a new small group (or if a new person comes to this meeting), see the listing of ice-breakers on page M7 of the center section.*

TO BEGIN THE BIBLE STUDY TIME
(Choose 1 or 2)

1. When you get lost are you more likely to stop and ask for directions or drive around until you find your way?

2. When, if ever, have you served on a jury? What was it like?

3. What was the best gift you ever received from your dad (or parents)?

READ SCRIPTURE & DISCUSS
(If you don't have time for all the questions in this section, conclude the Bible Study [30 min.] by answering question #7.)

1. What do you usually do when you see someone broken down on the side of the road?

2. Who is someone you appreciate because they accept you as you are?

3. In this passage what is Jesus calling for: No judgment? Self-judgment? Fair judgment? Divine judgment? Other?

4. When it comes to judging, who do you tend to judge hardest? Judge easiest?

Judging Others

7 *"Do not judge, or you too will be judged. ²For in the same way you judge others, you will be judged, and with the measure you use, it will be measured to you.*

³"Why do you look at the speck of sawdust in your brother's eye and pay no attention to the plank in your own eye? ⁴How can you say to your brother, 'Let me take the speck out of your eye,' when all the time there is a plank in your own eye? ⁵You hypocrite, first take the plank out of your own eye, and then you will see clearly to remove the speck from your brother's eye.

⁶"Do not give dogs what is sacred; do not throw your pearls to pigs. If you do, they may trample them under their feet, and then turn and tear you to pieces.

Ask, Seek, Knock

⁷"Ask and it will be given to you; seek and you will find; knock and the door will be opened to you. ⁸For everyone who asks receives; he who seeks finds; and to him who knocks, the door will be opened.

⁹"Which of you, if his son asks for bread, will give him a stone? ¹⁰Or if he asks for a fish, will give him a snake? ¹¹If you, then, though you are evil, know how to give good gifts to your children, how much more will your Father in heaven give good gifts to those who ask him! ¹²So in everything, do to others what you would have them do to you, for this sums up the Law and the Prophets."

5. What central truth about God does Jesus stress in verses 7–12? How have you experienced this in your life?

6. What grade would you give yourself for living by the Golden Rule (v. 12)?

7. What good gift would you like to ask of your heavenly Father?

CARING TIME

(Choose 1 or 2 of these questions before taking prayer requests and closing in prayer. Be sure to pray for the empty chair.)

1. If your group plans to continue, what would you like to study next (see inside the back cover for what's available from Serendipity)?

2. How has God been at work in your life this past week?

3. How can the group pray for you this week?

7:1–5 The "surpassing righteousness" of the members of the kingdom (5:20) is not to be license for a judgmental attitude toward others. In typical rabbinic fashion, Jesus lays down the principle (v. 1), provides a theological reason for it (v. 2), and then illustrates it (vv. 3–5).

7:1 *Do not.* This is a strong imperative meaning "Stop it!"

judge. In this context, this word refers to a condemning attitude that seeks to pass sentence upon the faults in others. This is not to say that disciples are never to make moral judgments about the actions of others (e.g., 7:15–20 requires them to do so in certain instances); rather, it condemns a harsh and censorious attitude toward others. Such an attitude would betray a lack of the personal brokenness and humility so central to the character of those who pursue God's kingdom (5:3,5).

7:2 *you will be judged.* While the normal human response to criticism is to criticize the one making the judgment, this phrase more likely refers to the fact that such an attitude sets one up to be scrutinized even more carefully by God in the final judgment.

the measure you use. This proverbial saying (see Mark 4:24 for its use in an entirely different context) was based on the rabbinic teaching that God would judge the world with two measures, one of justice and one of mercy. If one wished to be dealt with mercifully by God, then that person should deal mercifully with others (see also 6:14–15).

7:3–5 Jesus uses a vivid, humorous hyperbole (that also has its roots in rabbinic tradition) to express how hypocritical it is to judge the minor fault of another in the light of the enormity of one's own unrecognized sin.

7:4 *speck.* The word refers to something very small, like a splinter of wood or a bit of sawdust.

plank. The folly of trying to clear out a speck in another person's eye when one is blinded by a whole piece of wood in one's own is obvious.

7:5 It is not that the other person has no fault. There is a speck there. The problem is that people are more prone to notice the faults of others while they ignore the glaring difficulties and sins in their own lives.

hypocrite. See note on 6:2 (p. 36). The Pharisees are always in the background of the various teachings in this sermon.

7:6 While difficult to interpret, this brief parable (unique to Matthew) may have been intended as a balance to the command in verse 1. While a censorious, condemning attitude has no place in the life of a follower of Jesus, discernment and discrimination are needed. The issue in verses 1–5 is self-righteous judgment of others, not, as required here, a clear-headed sense of where others are in terms of their commitments.

what is sacred. It may be that what is meant here is the flesh of animals offered for sacrifice in the temple services. It would be unthinkable for a priest to carelessly toss such flesh to dogs, who would make no distinction between it and other carrion they might devour.

pearls. Something as precious as pearls would never be given to pigs. Not only would they be unable to appreciate their beauty, but they would trample them underfoot as something useless (since they are not edible). The early church interpreted the sacred food and the pearls as the Eucharist, which it forbade to those who were not baptized. Stott and others suggest that it is better to see the pearls and holy food as metaphors for the Good News of the kingdom of God. The disciples are not to continue to share precious spiritual truth with those who are unable or unwilling to see its value. To do so is only to invite blasphemy and abuse. This principle is seen in Jesus' words to the disciples when he sends them out to preach in Matthew 10:11–16.

dogs / pigs. The dogs here were wild, violent animals. Pigs were ceremonially unclean animals which Jews would neither eat nor raise (see 2 Peter 2:22). The type of people in view are those who have deliberately rejected the ways of God.

7:7–11 Jesus encourages his disciples to come to God in prayer continuously, in confidence that God is good and desires to meet their needs.

7:7 *Ask / seek / knock.* Each of these verbs is a present imperative, which means "keep on asking," "keep on seeking," and "keep on knocking." They should be read as three phrases, each emphasizing the same point ("to ask" is the same as "to seek" which is the same as "to knock"), rather than as a description of increased intensity in prayer.

it will be given / you will find / the door will be opened. The point of this verse is not that people will only be granted requests from God if they show increasing intensity in prayer (by first asking, then seeking, then knocking and demanding attention!), but to assure the disciples that God will indeed respond to the needs of those who pray.

7:9–11 Once again Jesus uses an analogy to make his point. The way a good father treats his child is how God treats his children.

7:9–10 bread / fish. The most common food in Galilee.

7:10 snake. This is probably an eel-like fish without scales that Jews were forbidden to eat (Lev. 11:12).

7:11 you are evil. This strong statement is meant to contrast the absolute goodness of God with the sinfulness that stains even the best of human parents. The point is that since usually not even human sinfulness will cause a father to deny food to his own son, how could one think that God would deny any good thing needed by those who call upon him?

7:12 This is the so-called Golden Rule. While it has no immediate connection to the teaching on prayer in verses 7–11, it does sum up what the righteousness of the disciples is to look like. It provides a foundational perspective on all human relationships. The negative form of this rule was widely known in the ancient world: "Do not do to others what you do not want them to do to you." Such diverse figures as Confucius and the great rabbi Hillel taught this. It is also found in Hinduism, Buddhism, as well as in Greek and Roman teaching. Jesus, however, alters this statement in a slight but highly significant way. He shifts this statement from the negative ("Do not") to the positive ("Do"). By so doing, he provided the world with one of the great (and rare) advances in moral understanding. Whereas the negative rule was fulfilled by inaction (not bothering others), the positive rule requires active benevolence (working for the good of others).

So. This links the Golden Rule to all the previous teaching in this section. This is the climax and summary of the Sermon on the Mount.

this sums up the Law and the Prophets. The Golden Rule succinctly defines the essence of what the Old Testament teaching about human relationships was meant to accomplish (see also Mark 12:30–31 and Rom. 13:8–10).

On Judging ...

"(A judgmental attitude) was something that troubled the early Church; and it has constantly troubled the Church of God ever since.

"What is this danger against which our Lord is warning us? We can say first of all that it is a kind of spirit ... a self-righteous spirit ... a feeling that we are all right while others are not. That then leads to censoriousness, and a spirit that is always ready to express itself in a derogatory manner. And then, accompanying that, there is the tendency to despise others, to regard them with contempt.

"It seems to me, further, that a very vital part of this spirit is the tendency to be hypercritical ... which means (someone who) delights in criticism for its own sake and enjoys it. ...

"It shows itself in a readiness to give judgment when the matter is of no concern to us at all. How much of our time do we spend in expressing our opinion about people who really have no direct dealings with us? ...

"A further way in which we may know whether we are guilty of this is to ask if we habitually express our opinion without a knowledge of all the facts.

"Another indication of it is that it never takes the trouble to understand the circumstances, and it is never ready to excuse; it is never ready to exercise mercy. (Someone) with a charitable spirit ... is prepared to listen and to see if there is an explanation ... to see if there may be mitigating circumstances. But the man who judges says, 'No, I require nothing further.'

"But perhaps we can end the description and bring it to its awful revolting climax by putting it like this: This spirit really manifests itself in the tendency to pronounce final judgment upon people as such ... it is not a judgment so much on what they do, or believe, or say, as upon the persons themselves. It is a final judgment upon an individual, and what makes it so terrible is that at that point it is arrogating to itself something that belongs to God" (D. Martyn Lloyd-Jones, *Studies on the Sermon on the Mount, Vol. 2,* Eerdmans, 1960, pp. 166–169).

12 Gates / Fruit—Matthew 7:13–23

THREE-PART AGENDA

ICE-BREAKER
15 Minutes

BIBLE STUDY
30 Minutes

CARING TIME
15–45 Minutes

LEADER: Has your group discussed its plans on what to study after this course is finished? What about the mission project described on page M6 in the center section?

TO BEGIN THE BIBLE STUDY TIME
(Choose 1 or 2)

1. What is your favorite kind of tree and why?

2. When on a narrow, windy road (with sheer drop-offs) are you more likely to close your eyes and pray or enjoy the view?

3. At the beginning of a movie, how can you tell who the "bad guy" is going to be?

READ SCRIPTURE & DISCUSS
(If you don't have time for all the questions in this section, conclude the Bible Study [30 min.] by answering question #7.)

Jesus begins the conclusion to the Sermon on the Mount by contrasting genuine commitment against mere formal commitment to his way.

1. When you were growing up, who did your parents warn you to stay away from? If you are a parent, who do (or did) you warn your children to stay away from?

2. Where do the roads in verses 13–14 lead? Which is the road less traveled and why?

The Narrow and Wide Gates

¹³*"Enter through the narrow gate. For wide is the gate and broad is the road that leads to destruction, and many enter through it. ¹⁴But small is the gate and narrow the road that leads to life, and only a few find it.*

A Tree and Its Fruit

¹⁵*"Watch out for false prophets. They come to you in sheep's clothing, but inwardly they are ferocious wolves. ¹⁶By their fruit you will recognize them. Do people pick grapes from thornbushes, or figs from thistles? ¹⁷Likewise every good tree bears good fruit, but a bad tree bears bad fruit. ¹⁸A good tree cannot bear bad fruit, and a bad tree cannot bear good fruit. ¹⁹Every tree that does not bear good fruit is cut down and thrown into the fire. ²⁰Thus, by their fruit you will recognize them.*

²¹*"Not everyone who says to me, 'Lord, Lord,' will enter the kingdom of heaven, but only he who does the will of my Father who is in heaven. ²²Many will say to me on that day, 'Lord, Lord, did we not prophesy in your name, and in your name drive out demons and perform many miracles?' ²³Then I will tell them plainly, 'I never knew you. Away from me, you evildoers!' "*

3. Who are the false prophets you need to be on your guard against? What "test" does Jesus give us for identifying them?

4. What are some of the "good fruits" Jesus is looking for (see notes on v. 16)? How can these fruits be cultivated in your own life?

5. How can someone do works in Jesus' name but not know him?

6. On a scale of 1 (rotten) to 10 (fully ripened), how did you feel about the fruit in your life this past week?

7. What can you do in the following week to cultivate good fruit?

CARING TIME
(Choose 1 or 2 of these questions before taking prayer requests and closing in prayer.)

1. Next week will be your last session in this study. How would you like to celebrate: A dinner? A party?

2. What is the next step for this group: Starting a new group? Continuing with another study?

3. How can the group pray for you this week?

Notes—Matthew 7:13–23

Summary. The Sermon on the Mount is concluded by another four sets of contrasts (see also 6:19–34) in which Jesus calls his disciples to genuine commitment over against mere formal commitment to his way. Having taught the way of surpassing righteousness (5:20), these four pictures call Matthew's readers to make a choice. In spite of all the apparent choices and opinions in the world today, these passages remind us that ultimately there are only two alternatives before us. There are only two ways (broad and narrow, vv. 13–14), only two kinds of teachers (false and true, 7:15–20), only two kinds of followers (doers and sayers, vv. 21–23), and only two kinds of foundations (rock and sand, vv. 24–27, see Session 13). The choice in each case is between the way of Christ and the way of the world.

7:13–14 The idea of two ways—the way of wickedness and the way of virtue—was taught by Greek writers (e.g., Hesiod), the psalmists (Ps. 1), and by Jewish prophets (e.g., Jer. 21:8).

7:13 *wide is the gate and broad is the road.* The wide gate and broad road, which is followed by most people, has been described throughout the Sermon. It is the way of life that stands in contrast to the values taught in the Beatitudes.

destruction. This is where the "natural" way leads. Jesus does not define this destiny, but the word he uses for it makes it clear that it is an awful end. While ultimately such a lifestyle leads to the destruction that is part of the wrath of God against sin (Rom. 1:18), it is important to keep in mind that a lifestyle marked by the broad way leads to destruction here and now, in the sense of estranged relationships and inner chaos. The broad way, while well traveled, is not particularly pleasant for those who choose it.

7:14 *small is the gate and narrow the road.* The narrower road is the way of life advocated in the Sermon. It is the way of humility, compassion, and justice pursued because one is loyal to Jesus as the Lord (5:3–12). It is the way of reconciliation, love, integrity, generosity and a love without boundaries (5:21–48). It is the way of inner devotion to God (6:1–18) marked by a wholehearted commitment to God and his ways (6:19–34). It is the way of mercy toward others (7:1–5), and trust in God's goodness (7:7–11). It is the way of actively seeking the good of others (7:12). This way is entered through a nar-

row gate which requires us to leave behind the baggage of prejudice, selfish ambition, pride and other loyalties. This way calls for discipline, training and faith. Such a decision calls for people to go against the sinful tendencies of the broad way that seem so natural. Therefore, it is chosen by fewer people.

life. The narrow way leads to life in all senses of the word. In this life, the narrow way leads to an inner wholeness marked by meaning and purpose (experienced through the presence of God), and to fulfilling relationships marked by integrity and harmony. It also is the way to eternal life with God, since it reflects the character of what that life entails. Jesus will refer to this destiny in verse 21 as "entering the kingdom of God."

few. When asked whether only a few will be saved, Jesus does not answer directly, but calls the questioner to pursue the narrow road (Luke 13:23–24). Jesus does not deal with theoretical abstractions, but calls upon individuals to make the choice to follow him.

7:15–20 Prophets were people who claimed to speak in the name of God. False prophets, whether motivated by a desire for power and prestige or a desire for money, were a problem in both Judaism and Christianity (see Deut. 13:1–5; Jer. 23:9–40; 2 Peter 2:1; 1 John 4:1–3). Their concern was for themselves, not for the glory of God nor the well-being of those whom they influenced.

7:15 *Watch out.* Once again the disciple is called upon to make a judgment about other people. In this case, it is necessary to discern who speaks truthfully and who speaks falsely about religious truth.

sheep's clothing. Prophets (like Elijah and John the Baptist) often wore animal skins (2 Kings 1:8; Matt. 3:4). People might dress in this fashion and (by doing so) claim to be prophets. Or looking at this another way, false prophets might claim to be sheep (an image used for disciples) or they might pretend to be as harmless as sheep, but their true nature is that of vicious wolves who want to feed off others. While the nature of the "dogs" and "pigs" (7:6) is obvious, these wolves are harder to detect, for their intentions and character are masked by outward appearances. Once again, Jesus probably has the Pharisees in mind here.

56

7:16a *By their fruit.* John Stott suggests three ways that the fruit of a Christian teacher is to be tested to see whether it is good or bad: "The first kind of 'fruit' by which false prophets reveal their true identity is in the realm of character and conduct. ... This being so, whenever we see in a teacher the meekness and gentleness of Christ, his love, patience, kindness, goodness and self-control, we have reason to believe him to be true, not false. On the other hand, whenever these qualities are missing, and 'the works of the flesh' are more apparent than 'the fruit of the Spirit'—especially enmity, impurity, jealousy and self-indulgence—we are justified in suspecting that the prophet is an imposter. ... A second 'fruit' is the ... actual teaching. ... The apostle John gives us an example of this, for the Asian churches to which he wrote had been invaded by false teachers. ... He encouraged them to (consider) whether the teachers' message was in accord with the original apostolic instruction, and in particular whether it confessed Jesus as the Christ come in the flesh (1 John 2:22–24). ... A third test ... concerns their influence. We have to ask ourselves what effect their teaching has on their followers. ... Its gangrenous progress is seen when it upsets people's faith (2 Tim. 2:18), promotes ungodliness (2 Tim. 2:16) and causes bitter divisions (1 Tim. 6:4; 2 Tim. 2:23)." It is on the basis of tests such as these that the church is to evaluate those who would be its leaders.

7:16b Jesus uses two illustrations to show that conduct demonstrates what is true about a person. False prophets will not produce fruit like grapes and figs that nourish people; instead they produce only thorns and thistles which cut and hurt.

7:21–23 Matthew continues to press home the meaning of discipleship by stressing the point that merely saying "Jesus is Lord" is not enough. Such an affirmation is shown to be genuine or false by what a person does. Actions demonstrate the reality of affirmations. Thus, on the Day of Judgment, the false prophets (and others) may protest that they ministered in Jesus' name, but the truth that they never knew him will be revealed.

7:21 *"Lord, Lord."* Such people claim allegiance to Jesus. The earliest Christian confession was "Jesus is Lord" (1 Cor. 12:3), but the fact is that those who do not do his will render this confession meaningless. Luke 6:46 expresses the same point even more succinctly: "Why do you call me 'Lord, Lord,' and do not do what I say?"

7:22 *on that day.* This is the Day of Judgment. Throughout the Bible, there is a clear expectation of a final accounting of humanity by God.

"Lord, Lord, did we not ... ?" Two important aspects of discipleship are accentuated in this verse: (1) Neither verbal allegiance to Jesus, nor powerful actions, nor success in ministry, nor the use of a certain type of "God-talk" can by itself be taken as evidence of a person being a true spokesperson for God. What really counts is whether that person is walking in the ways of God. (2) No one will enter the kingdom who attempts to do so on the basis of his or her deeds. These people tried to persuade the Lord to allow them access to his kingdom. The proper way to call upon Jesus as Lord is to acknowledge his sovereignty over all of one's life, look to him for mercy, and humbly live in accordance with his teachings.

13 Two Builders—Matthew 7:24–29

THREE-PART AGENDA

ICE-BREAKER
15 Minutes

BIBLE STUDY
30 Minutes

CARING TIME
15–45 Minutes

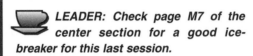 *LEADER: Check page M7 of the center section for a good ice-breaker for this last session.*

TO BEGIN THE BIBLE STUDY TIME
(Choose 1 or 2)

1. What's the worst storm you can remember?

2. What's something you built or made when you were young? Did it last?

3. How do you handle home improvement projects: Hire help? Do it yourself? Get friends to help?

READ SCRIPTURE & DISCUSS
(If you don't have time for all the questions in this section, conclude the Bible Study [30 min.] by answering question #8.)

The Sermon concludes with a parable presenting Jesus' listeners with a decision.

1. What is the immediate forecast for the "weather" in your life: Sunny? Overcast? Stormy? Other?

2. Who or what is the rock in your life—the person or thing you cling to in storms?

3. What two choices does Jesus present in this passage? What results come from these choices?

4. To be a "wise builder" at this point in your life, do you need to learn more or practice what you already know?

The Wise and Foolish Builders

24"**Therefore everyone who hears these words of mine and puts them into practice is like a wise man who built his house on the rock.** 25**The rain came down, the streams rose, and the winds blew and beat against that house; yet it did not fall, because it had its foundation on the rock.** 26**But everyone who hears these words of mine and does not put them into practice is like a foolish man who built his house on sand.** 27**The rain came down, the streams rose, and the winds blew and beat against that house, and it fell with a great crash.**"

28**When Jesus had finished saying these things, the crowds were amazed at his teaching,** 29**because he taught as one who had authority, and not as their teachers of the law.**

5. How would you describe your spiritual foundation: Shaky? Solid? Brand new? Slowly wearing away? Rebuilding?

6. How does the condition of your spiritual foundation now compare to what it was like before this course?

7. What "building materials" will you use in the coming weeks to build or maintain a firm foundation on "The Rock"?

8. What teaching from this study of the Sermon on the Mount most amazed and challenged you?

CARING TIME
(Choose 1 or 2 of these questions before taking prayer requests and closing in prayer.)

1. What was the high point or the "Serendipity" (unexpected blessing) for you in this group?

2. What has the group decided to do next? What is the next step for you?

3. How can the group continue to pray for you?

7:24–27 Both Matthew's and Luke's version of the Sermon conclude with this parable, which dramatically highlights the choice with which Jesus confronts his listeners. One must decide either to put his teaching into practice or else face the destruction that is the end result of any other choice. People in our culture do not like to be faced with such stark alternatives, especially in the area of religious belief. Jesus, however, clearly teaches that there is only one way of living that leads to life. He himself is the way, the truth and the life (John 14:6), and commitment to him and his teachings is the only way one can survive the judgment of God. All other choices lead to death. The two houses in this parable may look alike (the issue throughout verses 13–27 is the contrast between outward appearance and inner reality), but only the one built on a solid foundation (obedience to God) will stand when the storm (of God's ultimate accounting) comes.

7:24 *Therefore.* The parable concludes the argument presented in 7:13–23. The choices one makes about the path one travels (7:13–14), who one listens to (7:15–20), and how one lives (7:21–23) all boil down to the ultimate choice of whether or not a person will build his or her life upon the foundation of Jesus and his teachings.

like a wise man. In the Old Testament, the wise person is the one who chooses to center his or her life around the truth of God's character and Law (Ps. 111:10, Prov. 3:5–7; 9:10). In contrast, the fool is the person who (regardless of how intelligent he or she may be) assumes that there is no ultimate consequence of living life in disregard to God and the Law (Ps. 14:1; Prov. 14:16). In this parable, both kinds of people hear Jesus' words. The difference in their character is shown in how they respond to his teachings. "Both men ... are builders, for to live means to build. Every ambition a man cherishes, every thought he conceives, every word he speaks, and every deed he performs is, as it were, a building block. Gradually the structure of his life rises" (Hendriksen).

on the rock. Houses whose foundations were secured to bedrock would be able to survive a bad storm. In this context, the rock is Jesus and his teaching.

7:25 Palestine was dry most of the year. But in the autumn, rains came and flash floods swept down the ravines. What looks like a fine place to build a house in the dry season may become a raging torrent during flood season.

7:26 *on sand.* Building on sand is easier; if there is no settling of the land, nor any pressure of wind or water, the house will stand just fine.

7:27 *the rain came down, the streams rose, and the winds blew.* Ultimately, the image of a storm is used as a picture of God's coming judgment upon the world (Hab. 3:9–12). The Bible as a whole, as well as Jesus' teachings in particular, speaks clearly of God's judgment. It is in light of the inevitability of God's judgment that people are urged to repent and look to Christ as the one who will deliver them from this judgment. However, the rains and wind do not only represent the final judgment. They also represent the hardships in this life that fall upon both believers and nonbelievers. Believers are not promised that they will be sheltered from life's difficulties, but that they can have a foundation that will allow them to stand through such troubles.

it fell. There is no hope for a house built on sand when the flood waters erode away the very basis upon which it stands. Those whose life is built upon pride, power or possessions have no hope when confronted with realities that wipe these things away.

with a great crash. The fall of the house, a symbol of the person who lives apart from God's ways, is graphically presented. Such will be the fate of those who ignore the message contained within the Sermon. Matthew ends the Sermon with this stark warning and its implicit call to repent.

7:28–29 The crowds, present at the beginning of the Sermon (5:1–2), are again brought into the picture.

7:28 *When Jesus had finished saying these things.* This is Matthew's way of signaling the close of a major section of Jesus' teaching in order to make a transition to a new part of his narrative (see Matt. 11:1; 13:53; 19:1; 26:1).

amazed. The reaction of the crowds stresses the radically new message Jesus brought. He had shown that the kingdom belonged not to the Jews who would fight the Romans, but to all people who humbled themselves before God. He had shown that the Law which Judaism prized (as what set them apart from everyone else) really condemned them, since even their most zealous members (the Pharisees) had failed to embrace its teachings. He had pointed out a new way of living that called for a deep inner integrity, humility, graciousness and love. He repudiated the religious system for being concerned only with externals. He said there was no reward from God for that type of behavior. He forced people to seriously consider what truly motivated them. He stressed the need for a conscious decision to choose God's ways. All of this would cause his listeners to wonder who was delivering such a new, radical call requiring absolute allegiance to himself. The final effect of the Sermon on the Mount is to call attention to the one who gave this message. The real question Matthew leaves the reader with is, "How will I respond to this Jesus?"

7:29 their teachers of the law. Literally, "scribes," religious lawyers who interpreted Jewish law. Originally, it was their job to make copies of the Old Testament. Because of their familiarity with Scripture, people consulted them about points of law, and hence their role evolved into that of teacher of the Law. Their authority rested in their ability to quote the writings of earlier rabbis to prove their points. In contrast, Jesus' power lay in his message's implicit moral force and in the fact that he called upon no outside authority to validate his teaching.

Building Your House Upon a Rock

[The person who builds his or her house on the rock is the one who:]

"... allows every part of the Bible to speak to him ... he does not rush to a few favorite Psalms and use them as a kind of hypnotic when he cannot sleep at night; he allows the whole Word to examine him and search him. ... In other words, the true Christian humbles himself under the Word. ... the man who is right with respect to this Sermon is a man who, having humbled himself, submits himself to it, becomes poor in spirit, becomes a mourner for his sins, becomes meek because he knows how worthless he is. He immediately conforms to the Beatitudes because of the effect of the Word upon him, and then, because of that, he desires to conform to the type and pattern set before him. ... Any man who desires to live this type and kind of life is a Christian. He hungers and thirsts after righteousness; that is the big thing in his life. ... Observe the nature of the test. It is not asking whether you are sinless or perfect; it is asking what you would like to be, what you desire to be.

"... the true believer ... (is one whose) supreme desire is to do these things (in the Sermon) and be like the Lord Jesus Christ. It means he is a man who not only wants forgiveness, not only wants to escape hell and go to heaven. Quite as much, he wants positive holiness in this life and in this world. ... That is the man who builds upon the rock. He is a man who desires and prays for holiness and who strives after it. He does his utmost to be holy, because his supreme desire is to know Christ. ... to know Christ now, to have Christ as his Brother, to have Christ as his Companion, to be walking with Christ in the light now, to enjoy a foretaste of heaven here in this world of time—that is the man who builds upon the rock. He is a man who loves God for God's sake, and whose supreme desire and concern is that God's name and God's glory may be magnified and spread abroad.

"That is what is meant by practicing the Sermon on the Mount. If, on the other hand, you find that you cannot answer these tests satisfactorily, there is but one inevitable conclusion: you have been building upon the sand. And your house will collapse. ... You will see, then, that you have nothing. If you see that now, admit it, confess it to God without a second's delay. Confess it and humble yourself 'under the mighty hand of God.' Acknowledge it and cast yourself upon His love and mercy, tell Him that, at last, you desire to be holy and righteous; ask Him to give you His Spirit and to reveal to you the perfect work of Christ on your behalf. Follow Christ, and He will lead you to this true holiness, 'without which no man shall see the Lord' " (D. Martyn Lloyd-Jones, *Studies in the Sermon on the Mount*, Vol. 2, Eerdmans, 1960, pp. 312–314).

Caring Time

Acknowledgments

It is not possible (nor desirable) to tackle as formidable a subject as the Sermon on the Mount without the aid of others. The standard exegetical tools have, of course, been used: The Arndt and Gingrich *Greek-English Lexicon of the New Testament, The Interpreter's Dictionary of the Bible,* etc. In addition, reference has been made to a series of fine commentaries: Albright, W. F. and Mann, C.S., *Matthew (The Anchor Bible),* Doubleday, Garden City, NY, 1971. Betz, Hans Dieter, *Essays on the Sermon on the Mount,* Fortress Press, Philadelphia, PA, 1985. Bonhoeffer, Dietrich, *The Cost of Discipleship,* MacMillan Publishing Company, New York, NY, 1963. Bruce, F.F.,*The Hard Sayings of Jesus,* InterVarsity Press, Downers Grove, IL, 1983. France, R.T., *Matthew (Tyndale New Testament Commentaries),* Eerdmans, Grand Rapids, MI, 1985. Hendriksen, William, *The Gospel of Matthew,* Baker Book House, Grand Rapids, MI, 1973. Hill, David, *The Gospel of Matthew: The New Century Bible Commentary,* Eerdmans, Grand Rapids, MI, 1981. Kepler, Thomas (ed.), *The Fellowship of the Saints,* Abingdon Press, New York, NY, 1948. Lapide, Pinchas, *The Sermon on the Mount,* Orbis Books, Maryknoll, NY, 1986. Lloyd-Jones, D. Martyn, *Studies in the Sermon on the Mount,* Eerdmans, Grand Rapids, MI, 1960. Mounce, Robert H., *Matthew: A Good News Commentary,* Harper and Row, San Francisco, CA, 1985. Patte, Daniel, *The Gospel According to Matthew,* Fortress Press, Philadelphia, PA, 1987. Stott, John R.W., *Christian Counter-Culture,* InterVarsity Press, Downers Grove, IL, 1978. Vaught, Carl G., *The Sermon on the Mount: A Theological Interpretation,* State University of New York Press, Albany, NY, 1986.

Copyright Endorsements

Grateful acknowledgment is made to the following publishers for permission to reprint copyright material.

Session 1: Crosby, Michael, *Spirituality of the Beatitudes,* © 1981. Used by permission of Orbis Books, Maryknoll, NY.

Session 2: Stott, John R.W., *The Message of the Sermon on the Mount* © 1978 by John R.W. Stott. Used by permission of InterVarsity Press, Downers Grove, IL. Lloyd-Jones, D. Martyn, *Studies on the Sermon on the Mount, Vol. 2,* © 1960. Used by permission of Eerdmans Publishing, Grand Rapids, MI. Miller, Calvin, *The Singer* © 1975. Used by permission of InterVarsity Press, Downers Grove, IL.

Session 3: Stott, John R.W., *The Message of the Sermon on the Mount* © 1978 by John R.W. Stott. Used by permission of InterVarsity Press, Downers Grove, IL.

Session 4: Stott, John R.W., *The Message of the Sermon on the Mount* © 1978 by John R.W. Stott. Used by permission of InterVarsity Press, Downers Grove, IL.

Session 8: Stott, John R.W., *The Message of the Sermon on the Mount* © 1978 by John R. W. Stott. Used by permission of InterVarsity Press, Downers Grove, IL.

Session 9: Paternoster, James, "Materialism: Breaking Free From Madison Avenue's Grip," *Student Leadership Journal,* Fall, 1990. Used by permission of James Paternoster. Reprinted from *Rich Christians in an Age of Hunger,* © 1990, by Ron Sider. Used by permission of Word Incorporated, Dallas, TX.

Session 10: Foster, Richard J., *Celebration of Discipline* © 1978 by Richard Foster. Used by permission of HarperCollins Publishers.

Session 11: Lloyd-Jones, D. Martyn, *Studies on the Sermon on the Mount, Vol. 2,* © 1960. Used by permission of Eerdmans Publishing, Grand Rapids, MI.

Session 13: Lloyd-Jones, D. Martyn, *Studies on the Sermon on the Mount, Vol. 2,* © 1960. Used by permission of Eerdmans Publishing, Grand Rapids, MI.

Personal Notes